MAGIC

T0385516

HAU
BOOKS

www.haubooks.com

MAGIC
A THEORY FROM THE SOUTH

Ernesto de Martino

Translated and Annotated by
Dorothy Louise Zinn

Hau Books
Chicago

Cover and layout design: Sheehan Moore
Typesetting: Prepress Plus (www.prepressplus.in)

ISBN: 978-0-9905050-9-9
LCCN: 2014953636

Hau Books
Chicago Distribution Center
11030 S. Langley
Chicago, IL 60628
www.haubooks.com

Hau Books is marketed and distributed by The University of Chicago Press.
www.press.uchicago.edu

Contents

Translator's Note

Magic: A theory from the South is the second work in Ernesto de Martino's great "Southern trilogy" of ethnographic monographs, and following my previous translation of *The land of remorse* ([1961] 2005), I am pleased to make it available in an English edition. Whether in Italian or another language, a reader approaching the scholarly thought of de Martino for the first time is faced with no easy feat, and here as in the preceding volume I have attempted to guide the reader with annotations that help contextualize de Martino's concepts and terminology. Only occasionally do I suggest further sources; the literature of de Martino studies is dauntingly vast, but it is predominantly in Italian, so I have mostly chosen to limit such suggestions to what is available in English rather than provide an exhaustive referenced commentary to the text. Other than *The land of remorse*, the only monograph by de Martino currently available in English is his first treatise on magic, *Il Mondo magico* (1948, translated as *Primitive magic* [1972]), but due to some serious reservations I have about the approach utilized in that translation, I cannot endorse its usefulness.

This translation and its publication would not have been possible without the support of a number of friends and colleagues. Charles Stewart of University College London (UCL), a fellow anthropologist and translator of de Martino, helped get the ball rolling by mentioning this project to Giovanni da Col, Editor of Hau Books, who immediately took it on with the greatest enthusiasm. I consulted other colleagues to discuss issues of content in the translation: Sabina Magliocco and Fabio

Dei for hoary questions of magical terminology, and Ferdinando Mirizzi for references to Southern folklore. Lucanian scholar Angelo Tataranno, whose assistance proved invaluable for *The land of remorse*, continued to help me here with the utmost patience and generosity. Tony Molino and Luigi Zoja provided some specific indications with regard to psychiatric and psychoanalytic terminology. Preparation of the translation and annotations made use of research and exegeses of de Martino's corpus by Clara Gallini, George Saunders, Marcello Massenzio, Pietro Angelini, and a host of other colleagues too numerous to mention here. Pietro Clemente and Maria Minicuci have very kindly expressed their appreciation for my efforts in making such a sterling representative of Italian anthropology better known in the English-speaking world. Lia de Martino, Vera de Martino, and Vittoria de Palma have all encouraged this endeavor, as has Marcello Massenzio, President of the Associazione Internazionale Ernesto de Martino. I would also like to thank the Hau staff who have collaborated most closely with me in the publication process: Stéphane Gros, Michelle Beckett, and Sean Dowdy. A special word of acknowledgement goes to the Free University of Bozen-Bolzano and numerous colleagues there for providing a sound base for my work and an occasional pat on the back, and to Elisabeth Tauber for her fruitful anthropological exchanges. The University's *freundlich und übereffizient* Library system was instrumental in helping me obtain some existing English translations for various works cited by de Martino. Finally, I would like to thank my family: my mother-in-law, who still remembers the days in Lucania when "people thought everything was caused by magic," other *parenti* here in Italy and in the United States, my husband Antonio, and our daughters Odile and Pauline, perfect heirs to a very Demartinian rational-magic compromise.

Magic: A theory from the South presents ethnographic research from the Italian region of Lucania/Basilicata, an area that has been a home to me for over twenty years and holds a special place in the Italian anthropological tradition, in part due to this very book. Today's visitor will find a world that is entirely different from the one described by de Martino. Nonetheless, some of the cultural forms that de Martino discusses are certainly still present, at times quite recognizable but frequently also visible in new configurations, be they syncretisms embracing "esoteric operators" and New Age discourses, apotropaic and religious practices addressing moments of crisis, or cultural revivals such as the one currently turning the magical misfortune of an unnamable, witch-infested Lucanian village into a touristic destination. These are matters for further anthropological inquiry in order to clarify the extent to which there are still some continuities between magic and religion as discussed here and the mechanisms by which we face "crises of presence" in our modern society.

I dedicate this translation to Antonio, who introduced me to the magic of the South half a lifetime ago.

DOROTHY LOUISE ZINN
Bressanone/Brixen
April 22, 2014

Preface

The choice between "magic" and "rationality" is one of the great themes that gave rise to modern civilization. First signs of this choice appeared in certain motifs of Greek thought and Evangelical preaching, but it came to form the dramatic core of modern civilization with the passage from demonological magic to Renaissance natural magic, with the Protestant polemic against Catholic ritual, with the founding of the natural sciences and their methods, with the Enlightenment and its faith in a reforming human reason, and with the various currents of thought tied to the discovery of historical dialectic and reason. Within this framework, even the bloody era of the witch trials, as much as it might seem to have been a return to the demonological conception of medieval magic, indirectly refers to this underlying antimagic polemic that runs through the entire course of Western civilization. The modern nations making up the West are "modern" to the extent that they have participated earnestly in this multifaceted process. It is a process in which we are still involved, at least to the extent that—alongside our scientific techniques and an awareness of the human origin and destination of cultural values—we still place a spontaneous importance on the sphere of mythical-ritual techniques and the "magical" power or word and gesture.

This volume has undertaken a very modest and circumscribed task: it aims to offer a few indicative and programmatic suggestions for determining the degree and limits to which Southern Italian cultural life has consciously participated in this great option of modern civilization. In the pair "magic and the South," the term "South" obviously does not represent a merely geographical designation, but rather one that is also political and social. In their differences in cultural history, the city-states and lordships of the North and the Center, the Papal States, and the Kingdom of Naples all present shades and nuances of a religious life connected to their respective social and political histories. In this sense, one may legitimately speak of a religious history of the South as a religious history of the Kingdom of Naples—of a socially and politically defined formation, geographically demarcated between holy water and saltwater, between the Papal States and the sea. As a formation in a religious sense, too, it entails certain specificities: Southern Catholicism, for example, with its notes of gaudiness and exteriority and with its particular ceremonial and ritualistic flourishes, has repeatedly been an object of observation and has constituted one of the preferred targets of Protestant writers' anti-Catholic polemics.

As for its concrete execution, this study opens with an ethnographic exploration of some Lucanian survivals[1] of the crudest practices of ceremonial magic, with the intention of determining the structure of magical techniques, their psychological function, and the regime of existence that favors their continuation in one of the most backward areas of the South. The attention subsequently shifts to the relationship between these survivals and the hegemonic form of religious life: Catholicism with its particular magical and Southern cast. We will observe numerous links, passages, syncretisms, and compromises that connect extracanonical low magic with the modes of popular devotion and the liturgy's own official forms. The result is a panorama that at first appears extremely discontinuous, contradictory, and marked by a curious coexistence of elements. And yet, upon closer examination, the unifying theme holding together such heterogeneous elements will become evident: the demand for psychological protection in the face of both the extraordinary power of the negative in daily life and the narrow confines of "realistically" oriented, efficacious behavior. A third moment in the study analyzes the

---

1.   Although de Martino uses the term "survival" here, it should be noted that he did not subscribe to the evolutionist framework often associated with this notion in social science. The region of Southern Italy featured in this study has two official names, "Lucania" as well as "Basilicata." Contemporary readers will find "Basilicata" more commonly used, but its adjectival form is usually *lucano* ("Lucanian"). —Trans.

participation of Southern high culture in the antimagic polemic from which modern civilization arose. This participation featured aspects that were hegemonic on a European level with regard to the Renaissance natural magic's polemic against demonological magic, but it demonstrated instructive limits in the subsequent Enlightenment period, when the antimagic polemic entered into its most relevant form as a choice between magic and rationality, between exorcism and experiment, and between witchcraft and reforming science. A general limit is given by the very scanty participation of the Neapolitan Enlightenment in the explicit and fervid polemic against the most exterior and ritualistic features of the confessional religion, and the fact that in this religious sphere it limited itself to the political problems of the relationship between church and state. We find a more specific limit, but in some respects a particularly instructive one, in the formation of the ideology of jettatura[2]: an ideology of compromise—wholly irrelevant from a theoretical point of view— that exercised a substantial influence in the practical sphere of custom in Naples. Jettatura is not the same thing as dark binding [*fascinazione*] of the medieval period or of the period of the witch trials, nor even that of natural magic; rather, it is a compromise formation of elite origin that maintains a psychological disposition between the serious and the facetious, the scrupulous and the skeptical. As it was elaborated by some Neapolitan Enlightenment thinkers, the ideology of jettatura contrasts a human reason that consciously reforms and plans social life to the somewhat ironic figure of the jettatore. The latter is a person who unconsciously and systematically introduces disorder into the moral, social, and natural spheres of reality, and whose status in the world is that of someone who, owing to blind destiny, always makes things go wrong. This volume places these limits to the Neapolitan Enlightenment[3] in relation to what, comparatively and polemically, may be designated as the nonhistory of the Kingdom of Naples. The fact is that while the

---

2. Chapters 6, 7, and 8 in the second part of this book deal centrally with jettatura. As de Martino explains, jettatura has no exact translation in other languages, but the English-language reader may find it helpful to conceive of it as a form of jinx borne by the glance of the jettatore. "Jettatura" and "jettatore" will appear throughout this text without italics. The Italian pronunciation of "j" is that of an English "y." —Trans.
3. A typographical error in the original reads "illusionismo." —Trans.

Anglo-French Enlightenment arose and developed on the basis of a real, rationalizing force of a vigorous commercial and industrial bourgeoisie that operated in the framework of strong, expanding national monarchies, the Neapolitan Enlightenment did not benefit from the same conditions, and it was thus more reserved and indulgent toward the needs of psychological protection connected to magical-religious ritualism.

At first glance, the section devoted to low ceremonial magic in Lucania might seem disproportionately long within this work: in point of fact, however, it was necessary for this study to give particular attention precisely to documentary material of this sort. The low ceremonial magic that survives today in the South, the magical flourishes of Southern Catholicism, the hegemonic function of the various Portas, Brunos, and Campanellas[4] in the elaboration of Renaissance natural magic, and on the other hand, the nonparticipation of the Neapolitan Enlightenment in the explicit and fervid polemic against the magical and ritualistic features of the official religion, and the elaboration of the ideology of jettatura on the part of some Neapolitan Enlightenment thinkers at the end of the eighteenth century: all of these stand in a definite historical relationship to one another, and to determine this it was necessary to underline with a proper emphasis what we can still see today in Southern culture at the lowest and crudest levels. This lowness actually marks a limit that should be sought not in the stupidity or ignorance of the plebes, but instead in the hegemonic forms of cultural life themselves, and in the final instance in "high" culture itself.

There is yet another consideration behind the choice to give a particular emphasis to the low forms of ceremonial magic. Southern magic is not only formed by relics of archaic rituals that fall increasingly into disuse with each passing day, but also—as mentioned above—by the particular magical tone of Southern Catholicism: here, it is no longer possible to speak of tattered relics and forms of magical-religious life that have no present-day importance for all strata of Southern society. Here, precisely owing to their crudeness and elementary quality, the relics of low ceremonial magic more sharply reveal the structural and functional features of

---

4. The references are, respectively, to Giambattista della Porta (ca. 1535–1615), Giordano Bruno (1548–1600), and Tommaso Campanella (1568–1639). —Trans.

the magical moment—albeit one that has been refined and sublimated—
that we also find in Catholicism, especially in its Southern specificities
and nuances. Moreover, when we speak of "relics" of low ceremonial magic, we tend to imagine archaeological remains that survive in a state of
absolute isolation and in stark contrast with the rest of cultural life. This
isolation and contrast take place with respect to the modes of the modern
high culture with which we abstractly compare these low elements, while
the concrete reality of the matter is a different one. In the case at hand, we
have a precious opportunity for a concrete study of the magical-religious
dynamic in a specific society through the immediate connection of crude
"Lucanian magic" with various critical moments of existence and its in-
sertion in the lowest level of a series of degrees and interconnections that
have the Catholic cult as a reference point. Finally, I would like to underline the fact that the material relative to "Lucanian magic" in this volume
does not remain closed, inert, and opaque. In general, we cannot histori-
cize religious folklore in its isolation when it appears as a jumble of relics
that ethnographic analysis abstracts from the living whole of a particular
society. The religious-folkloric relic can nonetheless acquire historical
sense either as a documentary stimulus that helps us to understand the
bygone civilization of which it was once an organic part. Or it may serve
as a documentary stimulus that helps us to measure the internal limits
and the internal force of expansion of the current civilization in which it
is preserved as a relic. Beyond these two possibilities for apprehending it,
from a historiographic point of view religious-folkloric material remains
a sort of no man's land, where collectors of folk traditions can continue to
exert themselves industriously and those who are nostalgic for lost para-
dises can find something upon which to latch their romantic impulses.
In relation to this methodological point, the Lucanian folkloric material
has stimulated two distinct historical-religious studies: the first was on
ancient ritual lament, published as *Morte e pianto rituale nel mondo antico*
(de Martino 1958), and the second is contained in the present volume.
With the necessary methodological precautions, in *Morte e pianto ritual*
I took a particular element of Lucanian religious folklore—together with
similar Euro-Mediterranean folkloric data—as a particular documentary element for reconstructing the particular mode of cultural resolution
of the crisis of mourning that was expressed in ancient lament and was

hegemonic until the advent of Christianity. The present study instead intends to utilize the material regarding Lucanian magic as documentation that will help us to identify some forms of backwardness within Southern high culture in comparison to corresponding European levels.

The documentary material relative to the Lucanian survivals of the crudest forms of low ceremonial magic was collected directly by the author in the course of a series of ethnographic investigations carried out between 1950 and 1957.[5] In particular, the documentary material of the section "Magical life in Albano" was gathered by a team investigation in which Emilio Servadio and Mario Pitzurra actively participated, and which was generously supported by the Parapsychology Foundation of New York. Many thanks to Franco Pinna, Ando Gilardi, and André Martin for their intelligent collaboration with the photographic material utilized.

ERNESTO DE MARTINO

5.   In her extensive efforts at making material from the de Martino archives available, Clara Gallini has edited and published the fieldnotes from de Martino's Lucanian expedition in September–October 1952 (see de Martino 1995a). The volume features fieldnotes transcribed from the notebooks of de Martino and his companion, Vittoria de Palma, and Gallini's own introductory essay offers an excellent contextualization of the research project. Further background to the Lucanian fieldwork expeditions is available in de Martino (1996). Pietro Angelini's intellectual biography also provides information and bibliographic references regarding de Martino's research in Lucania in the 1950s (Angelini 2008). The book edited by Clara Gallini and Francesco Faeta (1999) is another resource, featuring essays on de Martino's fieldwork in Lucania and elsewhere in the South and photographs from various expeditions. —Trans.

PART ONE

Lucanian Magic

CHAPTER ONE

Binding

The fundamental theme of low ceremonial magic in Lucania is binding (in dialect: *fascinatura* or *affascino*). This term indicates a psychic condition of impediment or inhibition, and at the same time a sense of domination, a being acted upon by a force that is as strong as it is mysterious, one that totally removes a person's autonomy as well as his capacity for decision-making and choice. The term *affascino* also designates a hostile force circulating in the air, inhibiting or compelling. The image of tying up and of the bound person as "being tied up" is reflected in the synonymous term *attaccatura*, when it is used to refer to binding. In particular, "tied blood" [*attaccatura di sangue*] is a bond that is symbolically represented as blood that does not flow freely in the veins. Binding often features headache, sleepiness, weakness, slackened muscles, and hypochondria, but its characteristic feature is the experience of an indomitable and ominous force. Binding entails a binding agent and a victim, and when the agent takes human form, the binding appears as evil eye [*malocchio*]: an evil influence that arises from an envious glance (and thus *evil eye* is also called *envy* [*invidia*]), with various nuances that range from a more or less involuntary influence to a spell [*fattura*] deliberately cast with a specific ritual, and which can even be a particularly fearsome death spell [*fattura a morte*]. The experience of domination can reach the point that an abnormal personality more or less completely invades behavior, a personality that is in contrast with the community's accepted norms: the subject will no longer simply be bound, but *spiritato*, someone possessed and in need of an exorcism.

The treatment for *fascinatura* (or *affascino, attaccamento, malocchio, invidia,* or *fattura*) is based on the execution of a particular ritual by specialized magic practitioners. In Grottole, a woman suffering from a headache suspected to be resulting from a magical cause can, in some cases, treat herself: she places a drop of oil in a basin of water and watches to see whether or not the oil spreads. If it spreads, it is a case of *fascinatura*; if it does not spread, it is a common headache, for example from a head cold. If the *fascinatura* has been proven, the woman takes care to throw the water in the street in front of a person who happens to pass by, believing that the passerby takes the *fascinatura* upon himself by stepping into the water, thereby freeing the victim. For suspect headaches one usually turns to a healer:[1] here, too, there are particular signs for deciding whether or not the condition is magical. The healer begins by tracing a small cross with her thumb on the forehead of her patient and then recites the following formula:

[1] *Padre, Figlio e Spirito Santo*   (Father, Son, and Holy Spirit
    Fascinatura va' da là via   Binding go away from there
    Va' da affascinare N. N.   Don't bind N. N.
    ca è carne battezzata.   Because her flesh has been baptized.
    Padre, Figlio e Spirito Santo   Father, Son, and Holy Spirit,
    Fascinatura non scì più nante.   Binding don't go any further.)

---

1.   The term in the original Italian text is *rimediante*. Here, de Martino uses the feminine forms for both the healer and her patient, and this reflects a predominant female participation in these practices. Below, this magic practitioner is called a *fattucchiera*, a figure very much akin to the "cunning woman" described in other European contexts (cf. Wilby 2005; Magliocco 2009). I thank Sabina Magliocco for her generous insights and references on this subject. Rather than translate various terms for magic workers as "cunning folk," in many cases throughout this text I have chosen to maintain the original Italian terminology where I believe that it renders a local image or specificity, or where possible English equivalents are too loaded with other images or meanings. —Trans.

During the recitation the *fattucchiera* is immersed in a controlled oneiric psychic condition, and in this condition she identifies with her client's state of binding and suffers from it: the production of the oneiric state makes the *fattucchiera* yawn, the identification and suffering makes her shed tears: when the *fattucchiera* doesn't yawn or shed tears, it means that no binding is present to make her react; therefore the client is not bound, and her headache depends on something else. The *fattucchiera*'s yawning and tears are thus taken to be "signs" of binding. In Colobraro, however, people think that the *fattucchiera* may not yawn or tear because the binding person is more powerful than she, and thus impedes her magical exploration.

In Colobraro the *fattucchiera* contacted for the case goes silently to her pantry and takes nine pinches of salt and three smoldering coals from the hearth. She places all of this in a basin full of water, submerges her left hand in the water, and then massages the patient's forehead in the form of a cross, pronouncing the proper spell:

[2] *Affascine ca vaie pe' la via*   (Binding that moves along the road
     da N. N. Non ci ire   don't go to N. N.
     che è bona nata   who is well born
     battezzata,   baptized,
     cresimata.   confirmed.
     A nome de Ddie e de la   In the name of God and the
     Santissima Trinitate.   Holy Trinity.)

The formula is repeated three times, and each time closes with an Our Father, a Hail Mary, and a Glory Be.

In the treatment of *fascinatura* it is important to decide not only if magic is in fact at work, but also, in the event that it is, who the magical agent is. One practice in Colobraro clarifies how to obtain indicative signs to identify, at least very approximately, the perpetrator of a *fascinatura*. Called to the client's home, the healer goes silently to the pantry to take nine pinches of salt and three smoldering coals from the hearth and places all of this into a basin full of water. She then traces massages on the patient's forehead and signs of the cross, pronouncing this formula:

[3]   *Padre, Figlio e Spirito Santo*   (Father, Son, and Holy Spirit
       da Francesca non ci ire   don't go to Francesca
       che è bona nata   who is well born
       battezzata,   baptized,
       cresimata.   confirmed.
       A nome de Ddie e de la   In the name of God and the
       Santissima Trinitate.   Holy Trinity.)

She repeats the formula three times, closing each time with an Our Father, a Hail Mary, and a Glory Be.

In Colobraro, as in Grottole, the spell's recitation is carried out in a controlled oneiroid psychic state: however, yawning takes on a more precise revelatory meaning. If the *fattucchiera* yawns during the Our Father, it is a sign that the binding is the work of a man; if she yawns during the Hail Mary, it is a woman; and if the yawn occurs during the Glory Be, the perpetrator is a priest.

Some formulas against *fascinatura* have another structure: the first part indicates three means by which the binding has been produced: the eye (and thus the glance), the mind (malevolent thought), and ill will (envious intent); in the second part, these hostile forces are contrasted with the magical power of the Trinity, with the aim of "unbinding" the victim. This spell from Viggiano is typical:

[4]   *Chi t'ave affascinate?*   (Who bound you?
       L'uocchie, la mente e la mala   An eye, a thought, an evil will
       volontà chi t'adda sfascinà?   Who has to remove your binding?
       Lu Padre, lu Figliolo e lu   The Father, the Son, and the
       Spirito Santo.   Holy Spirit.)

The spell must be repeated three times, each time accompanied by the Credo, a Hail Mary and an Our Father. A nearly identical spell was recorded in Valsinni, where the informant gave us some important information: if you work on a man, the headache disappears right away, whereas a women is more "soggettosa," meaning difficult to cure, and the exorcism works on her more slowly.

In this type of spell, the three negative forces (glance, evil thought, and envious intentions) are opposed to other forces (the Father, the Son, and the Holy Spirit) that are presumed to be more powerful. At other times, however, we find the two eyes that carried out the enchantment on the side of the negative forces, and on the side of the positive, there are not only more powerful forces but also more numerous ones. A spell from Savoia goes as follows:

[5] *Duie uocchie t'hanno affise*   (Two eyes stared at you
    tre te vonno aità   three want to help you
    Sant'Anna, Santa Lena   St. Anne, St. Lena,
    Santa Maria Maddalena.   St. Mary Magdalene.)

Additionally, one murmurs:

[6] *Scende la Madonna co' le*   (The Madonna comes down with her
    mane santé   holy hands
    in nome del Padre Figliuolo e   in the name of the Father, the
    Sprito Santo.   Son, and the Holy Spirit.)

In general these spells against binding encapsulate an exemplary myth of the binding's removal, and the "word" spoken and the "gesture" performed in the rite are effective inasmuch as they repeat and re-present a metahistorical model of removal, be it the exhibition of a baptismal immunity, the three binding elements that have been weakened by the Trinity, or the two envious eyes dealt with effectively by the three saints. In other cases, the model of removal becomes an explicit *historiola*: through the ritual word and gesture, it reabsorbs in its *exemplum* the current negativity of feeling bound. In a spell from Valsinni, the *exemplum* is Jesus' baptism:

[7] *A la funtana di Gisatte*   (At Jehosephat's fountain
    ddò fu battiate 'o figlie di   where the son of God was
    Ddie   baptized
    Vergine 'a Madre e vergine 'o   A virgin mother, a virgin
    Figlie   child
    Fa passare 'o male de ciglie.   Make the headache go away.)

CHAPTER TWO

Binding and eros

The magical possibility of binding and being bound has its elective terrain in erotic life, but while spells against evil eye and envy attempt to construct a defense against the evil energy that threatens people and their possessions, love spells are generally used to bind the beloved with an invisible and irresistible tie. Even men use such spells: in Ferrandina, to ensnare the woman he loves, a man places a wool braid in his mattress. Because of their greater social freedom, however, men can entrust the success of their plotting to more realistic means, to more normal forms of courtship, or the serenade. Because of their condition as the traditionally passive element in love affairs, and due to the rigor of custom that prevents them from undertaking realistic initiatives in this sphere, women turn more easily to the little world of magical conspiracies, love potions, premonitory or divinatory practices; in any case they remain connected to that world longer and more tenaciously then men do. A woman must make every effort to enchant a man: if the spell is not successful right away, she will have to repeat it for months and months, but always in odd numbers, until her man gives in. Menstrual blood, vaginal fluid, hairs from armpits and the pubis, blood from the veins all have greater power to bind [*legare*] and to attract, to pry a desired male away from a rival. Besides the usual potions with drops of menstrual blood in wine, coffee, broth, or other drinks, other potions may be used that are duly consecrated. In

Colobraro, a powerful love potion is made from the following recipe: the little finger of the right hand is tied and pricked and three drops of blood are drawn; a lock of hair is cut from the armpits and pubis; the hairs are mixed with the blood and the mixture is dried in the oven. This yields a powder that is brought to church to be consecrated during Mass. At the moment of the Elevation, one murmurs the following:

[8]   *Sanghe de Criste*   (Blood of Christ,
      demonie, attaccame a chiste   demon, tie me to this one
      Tante ca li è legà   you must bind him so hard
      ca de me non s'avì scurdà.   that he won't be able to forget me.)

In this way, the powder gets consecrated through the magic power of the high point of the Mass, and it is thus ready for use at the first favorable opportunity. Since menstrual blood is not always available when there is the chance to place it in a drink, one technique in Colobraro is to soak a rag with it, drip it into a bottle, and pronounce the following consecration spell:

[9]   *Sanghe della mia natura*   (Blood of my nature
      sine a la selbetura.   until burial.)

The bottle is kept aside and is used when needed.

Aside from potions inspired by a wholly transparent sexual symbolism, there are others that use the technique of knotting as a symbol of binding. In a major festival in Grottole, when a church bell rings, a person takes an "unmeasured ribbon" and repeats "some words" three times (a spell, which in this case our informant refused to provide): each time a knot is placed in the ribbon. In Viggiano, again during festivals, a person takes an "unmeasured" ribbon and makes three knots, repeating with each knot:

[10] *Io ti amo e ti rispetto*   (I love you and respect you
      come al sangue mio   like my own blood.
      Tu se traditore: You're a traitor:
      io ti attaccherò.   I'm going to bind you.
      Io ti attache a o' sanghe.   I'm binding you in blood.)

At this point, one makes a sign of the cross, and then very intently says: "I'm binding you in blood"—that is, precisely at the root of a person, which blood symbolizes. One closes with an Our Father, an Ave Maria, and a Gloria.

The theme of binding as evil eye or envy recurs with regard to weddings and the consummation of a marriage. In order to elude the evil forces threatening a couple, in Viggiano and in Savoia the wedding cortège cannot follow the same road on the way to and from the church. In Colobraro—and in Marsico Vetere—the bride and groom must jump over the threshold of the church, otherwise they may be attacked by a spell: in fact, on the threshold there might be a lace, knots, or other magical obstacles intentionally placed by some male or female specialist in spells. In Colobraro, the bride and groom must not dip their hands in the holy water font, for fear that it might contain some dissolved enchanted powder that has the effect of preventing consummation. During Mass, the couple's fortune is divined according to the gospel that is read: only that of Saint John is supposed to bring good luck to the newlyweds, less so Saint Mark and Saint Matthew, while Luke creates a veritable panic among the audience. At the end of Mass, newlyweds and relatives often crowd around the priest who officiated, and ask anxiously: "Which Gospel came out?" And the priest, who knows his parishioners' belief, calms them down by replying, "Saint John, Saint John," even if it is not true. During the celebration of Mass, the bride will take care to leave an edge of her wedding veil below the groom's knee: both the groom and the relatives will be quite careful to draw favorable or unfavorable omens according to how the Mass proceeds. Thus, for example, if a candle goes out on the bride's side, her luck will be bad, while the groom will have bad luck if a candle goes out on his side. But the riskiest moment magically, the one most in need of protection, happens when the newlyweds are getting ready to consummate the marriage. In Grottole, the parents of the two newlyweds prepare the wedding bed placing a rag under the pillow (or in the night table)—that serves to prove the bride's virginity—and some traditional instruments for fighting off evil eye, for example, six grains of wheat, a pinch of salt, open scissors, and a sickle. Additionally, the bed must not have been "seen" (looked at) by anyone except for the parents, again due to evil eye. When the couple retires to the bedroom, two men, one for the bride and one for the groom, keep a vigil outside the door and prevent anyone from doing *lu strite*: a magical conspiracy against the newlyweds to disturb their first night, and this consists in placing a plow or an animal's carcass outside the door. In Grottole, again, the bride's mother-in-law knocks on the wedding bed-chamber the morning after: if the groom tells her to come in, it means that the marriage has been consummated, but if he says "come back later," then it is a bad sign, and there is a strong presumption that the outcome has not been good. If everything has gone well, the mother-in-law enters into the bedchamber and inspects the rag to check for signs of lost virginity. In Pisticci, too, protective measures are taken against the magical risks of the first night: pins on the four sides of the bed, sickle and scissors under the mattress. With the same aim, in Colobraro one hides under a mattress a sickle, open scissors, a sieve (which suggests the idea of holding back the evil force), a piece of bell rope (which is an instrument for escaping binding, since it requires counting how many times the rope has pulled the bell to sound it). In Valsinni, a written letter (or a newspaper) substitutes the bell rope in its apotropaic function: the idea is that the elusive power of writing lies in the fact that the binding will be busied reading the handwritten or printed letters, which—in the experience of reading that semi-illiterate people have—requires a great deal of time and energy. According to an informant from Viggiano, the bride's bed is prepared with a sickle, scissors, and bits of newspaper, to which one adds the placing of a broom behind the door so that the binding, busied counting the strands of the broom, wastes time and gets discouraged or is surprised by the dawn, which is not propitious for its action. Finally, in Grottole, a plowshare under the bed guarantees the marriage's fertility.

With regard to a particular uncertain perspective, love magic takes on the form of a binding of the future, as in divinatory practices or in the exploration of signs. Thus, for example, according to information by a woman from Grottole, in order to learn whether or not a faraway lover is alive or dead, faithful or unfaithful, about to return or not, the lover awaits midnight of a Wednesday or a Friday, lights two candles in front of the good night angel, and murmurs the following spell:

[11] *Santa Monica pietosa*   (Pitiful Saint Monica
      Santa Monica lacrimosa   Tearful Saint Monica
      a levante andasti   You went to the east
      a ponente venisti   You came to the west
      come hai visto l'affetto di tuo just as you saw your son's
      figlio   affection
      così fammi vedere l'affetto di ... show me the affection of . . .)

Having recited the formula, the lover goes to the window and observes the signs that reach the town in the dark. Favorable signs are the sound of a bell (which means that the person is alive, or a return is near), a dog's howl (faithfulness), or a man passing (return). Alternatively, ill-omened signs are blowing wind (distancing), the echo of a couple's dispute (disunity), the rustling of running water (tears, blood). Divinatory practices must be concluded with three Credos, seven Our Fathers, seven Glorias, and a Saint Expeditus.

CHAPTER THREE

The magical representation of illness

As stated previously, the ideology of binding is the fundamental theme of low ceremonial magic in Lucania, in the sense that the other forms of magic are psychologically connected to the experience of domination lying at the basis of binding. In conditions of psychological misery,[1] any manifestation of negativity bears the risk of an even more serious negativity: a drop in the very moral energy of decision and choice, the loss of individual presence.[2] An organic disease, a death, uncertain prospects

---

1. Here and elsewhere in his discussions of the peasant regime of existence in Lucania, de Martino employs French psychologist Pierre Janet's expression *misère psychologique;* de Martino's posthumous work *La fine del mondo* contains a more direct treatment of Janet (de Martino 1977). —Trans.

2. The concept of *presence* [*presenza*] is central to de Martino's understanding of magic, but also of myth, ritual, and human culture more generally. As Adelina Talamonti and Roberto Pàstina have observed, de Martino developed this concept from his encounter with Pierre Janet's notions of "misère psychologique" and "présentification" (see Talamonti 2005; Pàstina 2005). de Martino applied Janet's insights to the so-called primitive world in the attempt to understand the role of magic, but in the post-World War II period in which he extensively engaged existentialist thinkers, he began to think of "presence" in more fundamental, ontological terms in relation to human existence *tout court*. As it took shape, in fact, de Martino's notion of "presence" as "being there" [*esserci*] has direct connections with Heidegger's

with regard to the necessities of life—these are all misfortunes to be dealt with through realistically oriented behaviors: but the worst misfortune arises when the very possibility of behaving is threatened. This is a risk signaled by the intervention of the sense of domination by an obscure, binding force that leaves individual presence without any margin for autonomy. The low ceremonial magic of Lucania appears to work on an imaginary level to fight specific manifestations of negativity that punctuate existence: in point of fact, though, it protects individual presence from the risk of not being able to preserve itself in the face of particular manifestations of negativity. Relatedly, the magical representation of illness gets confused with feeling dominated by obscure forces, and the magical representation of healing with feeling cured. In Colobraro, among "magical" headaches—those needing a magical treatment—there is one called *scindone* that is connected to the sun in the emotional classification of popular medicine. The connection has an objective basis in the fact that this headache has its onset at sundown after a day of laboring in the fields, and it stays with the sufferer for the entire night, making it impossible for him to sleep and rest. In the morning the painful headache continues to hold the sufferer's head in a vice, and a distressing prostration numbs his limbs. It is nonetheless necessary for the sufferer to head back out to the fields for his strenuous work, so as soon as the sun rises, the peasant stands before the morning star, opens his arms, and murmurs the following:

[12] *Buon giorno santi sole*   (Good morning, holy sun
      a li piedi del Signore   at the feet of the Lord
      da lu petto ne leva l'affano   remove the chest's panting
      da la testa lu gran dolore.   from the head, the great pain.
      Buon giorno, santi sole!   Good morning, holy sun.)

Dasein. Progressively elaborating this concept throughout his career, de Martino posited that this presence can enter into crisis and be threatened: in the midst of the crisis of presence, the sufferer loses her capacity for being-in-the-world, regressing to a passive, objectified state. As we see in the discussion in Part II of the present volume, de Martino views magic and ritual as cultural techniques for securing this threatened presence. On these points, readers may find Fabrizio Ferrari's (2012) overview in English useful. —Trans.

In Pisticci, the Colobraro *scindone* takes the name of *o'chiuve* (sun nail), and the spell for warding it off is the following:

[13]   *Buon giorno cumpà sole*   (Good morning my old friend sun
       e pe' Sante Salvatore   through the Holy Savior
       falla passà chiuve e dolore   make the nail and pain go away.
       Padre, Figliuole e Spirito Santo.   Father, Son, and Holy Spirit.)

The pagan-Catholic syncretism of these spells is evident: the Colobraro spell humiliates the Holy Sun at the feet of the Lord, and the one from Pisticci eliminates the epithet of Holy given to the sun and substitutes it with "old friend." In other spells against sun nail, the pagan-Catholic syncretism creates a parallel between the rising sun, the resurrection of Christ, and the disappearance of the headache, as in this spell from Ferrandina:

[14]   *Lévati cigghie come se leva*   (Remove yourself, headache, as
       o' sole   the sun rises,
       Come se leva Ddie Sante   as God the Holy Savior rises up.)
       Salvatore.

In another version from Ferrandina, the *historiola* narrates the birth and crucifixion of Jesus. In this case, the parallel is between the rising sun (*l'alzarsi del sole*), the rising (*innalzamento*) of Jesus on the cross, and the rising (*alzarsi*, going away) of the headache:

[15]   *Bella città di Betlemme*   (Beautiful city of Bethlehem
       Addò è nato nu belle figghiuolo. where a good son was born.
       Vergine a madre, vergine o   Virgin the mother, virgin the
       figghie: son:
       Alzate ciggie come jalza o sole   Get up and go, headache, like the
                                           sun rises
       Come jalzaie a la croce nostro   like our Lord was raised on
       Signore.   the cross.)

In all of these cases, a headache due to binding and a sun headache are mixed together: but the fusion takes place because of a common experience of domination perpetrated by occult forces. On the other hand, since through this common experience all illnesses have to do with bind-ing, it happens that spells can undergo frequent displacements in their use. Thus, for example, in Ferrandina the following spell, useful for mi-graines, can also be used for nettle rash:

[16] —*Male viente da dò viene?*   (—Bad wind, from where do you come?
    Male viente a dò vai?   Bad wind, where are you going?
    Vado sopa a N. N.   I'm getting on N. N.
    Sopa a N. N. non pote scì   You can't get on N. N.
    chedda è carne vattesciata   because his flesh is baptized
    A scì ndo nu vosche streme   I have to go to a faraway forest
    dò non se séntene   where you can't hear
    né campane de sunà   church bells ringing
    né cristiane de passà   nor people passing by,
    né gale de cantà!   nor roosters crowing!)

Here, the "bad wind" is represented in the same way as a binding that "moves through the roads" looking for victims. In its use against net-tle rash, the spell is preceded by a specific ritual: the sufferer wears her clothes inside-out for three days (so as to indicate the expelling of the evil force), then she goes to a *fattucchiera* who rubs her body with holy water while reciting the spell. The same spell exists in Pisticci in a sim-pler form and is used exclusively for specific skin conditions:

[17] *Male viente maledette*   (Damned evil wind
    e vattine a mare a necà   go drown yourself in the sea
    ca sta carne benedetta   because this is blessed flesh
    non hai cosa le fa.   you can't do anything to it.)

Having pronounced these words, the sufferer removes her clothes and leaves them at a crossroad where the first passerby will absorb the evil force pervading them. This version from Savoia is also simple:

[18] *Fui male vinte*   (Go away, evil wind
    da sop'a quest'anima innocente   from this innocent soul
    ind'a lu vosche oscure   into the dark forest
    addò non c'è luce e lume.   where there is neither light nor lan-tern.)

In a version collected in Oppido, a spell against evil wind is used to combat binding and enchantment:

[19] *Che Ddie e che Maria*   (With God and with Maria
    e le quatt'angole de la casa   and the four angles of my home
    male vinte non ce trase   evil wind do not enter
    nfacce a mme non s'accoste   don't come near my face
    né la dì né la notte   neither day nor night
    né a lu puntu de la morte   nor at death's door
    Vattinne, male vente triste   Go away, evil, wicked wind
    ca te caccie Gesù Criste   because Jesus Christ is chasing you
                              away

    Vu' siete cacciate   You're being chased off
    da la Santissima Trinitate   by the Holy Trinity
    Vattinne male vinte   Go away, evil wind
    Vattinne 'n guisa de vinte   Go the way of wind
    Vu' site cacciate   You're being chased away
    da la Santissima Trinitate   by the Holy Trinity
    Sciativenne 'ncompagnia   Go away in company
    va caccia Madre Maria   Mother Maria is chasing you away
    Male vinte brutta bestia   Evil wind, ugly beast
    vattinne da 'ncudde a chesta   get off of her back
    sciativenne, scumbinatoria   go away, disorder
    Male viente e male frutte   Evil wind and evil fruit
    vattinne da do sì venute,   Go back to where you're from,
    ca tu sì cacciate   because you're being chased away
    da la Santissima Trinitate.   by the Holy Trinity.)

In the Oppido version, too, whose use is effective against binding, the victim must remove her clothes and then put them back on inside-out; then, walking backward, she must leave the house and place the clothes outside the door, in the open air. The next morning, again walking backward, she must take them back and dress with them on the right side, taking care to repeat both the oration and the expellant procedure for three nights in a row.

In this magical conception of illness as binding or as "something done," the character of the symptom, the etiology of the illness, its diagnosis and therapy in the scientific, medical sense are all an entirely secondary matter: the most prominent aspect is instead "feeling acted upon" or "dominated" by the illness's occult force and the desire to feel released from this domination.

Because of their orientation, magical practices are "impervious" to what we consider to be magic's "defeats." In a psychological-protective sense, magical practices are always successful for those who are engaged in them, and in a psychosomatic sense they can also facilitate healing. But what keeps magic going is the regularity of its psychological-protective sense and not the exceptional or irregular quality of actual organic cures. Thus we may better understand the structure and function of a vast number of healing techniques of Lucanian low ceremonial magic. In Savoia, to cure "air fever" you take a string of black yarn and make a knot while murmuring the following:

[20]   *T'attacchi quartane*   (I'm tying you quartana
      terzana   terzana
      e freve d'aria   and air fever.)[3]

The knot must be started with the first verse and finished on the second; on the third verse the hand is detached from the finished knot. Then the string is folded and a knot is made in the center, and the same formula is repeated. Finally, a knot is made at the other end, the formula is repeated, and the string is slung across a bare shoulder and left there until it falls off. Malarial fevers (or those thought to be) are also treated with a similar technique. In Colobraro, a person collects urine in a small pan, and then, at dawn of the third day, leaves the house while holding the pan behind his or her back and walks backward with his or her back to the rising sun. At a certain point, without turning around yet, the pan's contents are thrown toward the sun, and the following is murmured:

[21]   *Sante Toma d'alto mare*   (Saint Toma of the high seas
      famme passà freve, fridde   make my fever, cold, and
      e quartane   quartana pass.
      'A prima domenica ca vene The first Sunday that comes
      non voglio provà pene   I don't want to suffer.)

---

3. *Terzana* and *quartana* refer, respectively, to cycles of malarial fever lasting three or four days. —Trans.

For a swollen spleen, in Colobraro you work with a "measureless" length of black wool yarn folded into three portions: then you use it to draw a sign of the cross on the spot where pain is felt, accompanying the gestures with the following formula:

[22] *Meveze e mevezone*   (Spleen and big spleen
    vattine al tuo cantone: go back to your canton
    e meveze e mevezone   spleen and big spleen.)

With the first verse of the spell, you stretch out the yarn, tracing one arm of the cross; with the second verse, you trace the second arm of the cross; and with the third, you make a knot that symbolizes the magical "tying up" of the evil. You repeat the procedure nine times, reciting an Our Father each time.

The traditional use of silver and gold for erysipelas has been widely documented. One spell from Grottole is as follows:

[23] *Je te 'ncanto resipla*   (I enchant you, o erysipelas
    sei rossa come 'na rosa   you're red as a rose
    pungente come 'na spina   prickly as a thorn
    'n nome di S. Nicola   In the name of St. Nicholas
    je te passe argente e oro   I pass silver and gold on you.)

While you recite this spell—which opens with the sign of the cross on the affected area—you rub the skin first with a silver ring and then a gold one, and you repeat the entire procedure three times.

In Savoia two different versions were recorded; the first one goes like this:

[24] *Fuie resibla*   (Go away erysipelas,
    ca l'argento vene   since silver is coming
    a chidde arte mare   in high seas
    e non riturnà più.   and don't come back again.)

You repeat the formula nine times and each time close with an Our Father; at the end of the entire series, you say nine Our Fathers and nine Ave Marias "presented in the name and glory of the eternal Father." The second version from Savoia is as follows:

[25] *Fuie resibla*   (Go away erysipelas
ca l'argento mo vene   since silver is coming now
L'argento è venuto   The silver has come
e tu te ne sì fuiuto   And you've escaped
a gàvete mare.   to high seas.
Non possa venì né mo né mai. May you not return, now or ever.)

In Tricarico, the spell orders the erysipelas to last no longer than a week, from one Friday to another:

[26] *Resipela cannaruta*   (Piggish erysipelas
o' venerdì si inzuta   You came on a Friday
o' sabato nasciuta   Saturday you were born
o' venerdì ti ni si sciuta   On Friday you went away.)

When someone gets something in his eye, or his eyes suffer from a draft, this well-known spell is used in Grottole:

[27] *Santa Lucia minze o' mare steva*   (Saint Lucy was in the middle of the sea
pponte d'altare recamava   she was embroidering altar lace.
Passò o figghiuolo de Maria   Maria's son passed by:
—Dimme, ce fa do, beata Lucia?   —Tell me, what are you doing here, blessed Lucy?
—Ce vol'esse maestro mio?   —What am I supposed to do, my master?
Na furia a l'uocchie m'è calata: Blood has gone into my eyes:
non pigghie ripose non notte non dì   I don't get rest day or night.

—Va' al mi' orto, ca ngè pove è finocchie: —Go to my garden, there's some fennel powder:
co le mie mane l'agghie chiantate;   I planted it with my own hands,
co le mie pede l'agghie pestate;   I pounded it with my own feet
e co le mi' uocchie l'agghie benedisciute. And I blessed it with my eyes.)

In Viggiano, the *historiola* instead involves St. Peter:

[28] *S. Pietro po' mare sciva*   (St. Peter was going by sea
      'na tavula de nave fategava   and was working a ship plank
      Na scerda ci arrivulava   A splinter flew off
      int'a l'uocchie ci ganzava   And went in his eye.
      Tutte l'uocchie nsanghinate: With bloody eyes
      vedette che 'ncera l'erba   He saw an herb
      chiamata virurella.   called *virurella*.[4]
      Tri volte pi' l'uocchie ti la passa, Pass it three times on your eyes,
      tutti i nervi si rinfriscano.   all the nerves are refreshed.)

You close this with an Our Father, an Ave Maria, and a Gloria. The formula is recited three times at sunset.

For a stomach ache (*male de ventre, rògliere*) the spell is based on the following *historiola*: once upon a time a saint who wandered incognito (in some versions it was Jesus himself) asked for hospitality in the home of a married couple. The husband was gracious but his wife shirked the duty of hospitality and was rather rude to the wanderer. The saint punished her with a stomach ache, but then, thanks to her husband's intercession, he cured her by reciting a spell that gently alluded to the shabby treatment he received:

[29] *Buon uomo, cattiva donna*   (Good man, bad woman
      Buona accoglienza, mala   Good hospitality, bad
      accoglienza   hospitality
      Scurze de pane bruciate   Burned bread crusts,
      vine annacquate   watered-down wine,
      lu pesce a la fenestra   fish in the window,
      paglia ampossa   wet straw.
      Vattinne rògliere ra N. N.   Go away, ache, from N. N.
      Come non gi fusse.   As if nothing had happened.)

The allusion is obvious: the pilgrim recalls the rude actions aimed at him, the burned bread crust, the watered-down wine, wet straw, fish taken away and placed on the window sill. Even so, this version, which is from

---

4. The medicinal herb is *anthyllis vulneraria*, also known in English as kidney vetch or woundwort. —Trans.

Savoia, lacks the true *historiola* that instead appears in the following version from Stigliano:

[30] *Sante Martine da Roma venia*   (St. Martin came from Rome
    tutte mpasse ca forte chiuvia   all wet since it rained hard
    sceve dicenne l'Ave   he went around saying the Hail
    Maria.   Mary.
    Arrivate a na casa   The husband wanted, the wife
    nova.   didn't.
    Pesce cutte se mangiai   He ate cooked fish
    'Nzott'acqua, sopa sarmente   over water over vine shoots
    fa passà stu dolore de ventre.   Make this stomach ache go away.)

In this version from Viggiano, Jesus himself takes the place of St. Martin:

[31] *Quanne Criste cammenava*   (When Christ was walking
    dodice apostole portava.   he brought along twelve apostles.
    N'ommene rabbene, na femmene   A good man, a bad woman,
    malamente,   water under and vine shoots above:
    acqua sotto e 'ncoppa sarmente: the stomach ache goes completely
    passa tutto o' male de la ventre   away.)

Here is another version from Viggiano:

[32] *Gesù Cristo a Roma venia*   (Jesus Christ came from Rome
    a la taverna scette a alluggià   he went to lodge at the tavern.
    Spina de pesce à ra mangià   He has to eat fish bones,
    fuche stutate pe' se caliendà   the fire for heating was out:
    stu male de ventre te pozza passà.   May your stomach ache go away.)

Among magical illnesses, the traditional ideology of *male dell'arco* (jaundice, literally "arch disease") occupies a prominent place. According to this ideology, the yellow is absorbed by the sufferer when he urinates against a rainbow, since in order to heal, it is necessary to be freed of the blood's yellow malignancy. In Pisticci, before sunrise and without uttering a word to anyone and without replying if questioned, the sufferer leaves his house and passes under three masonry arches, repeating this spell three times for each arch:

[33] *Buon giorno, cumpà arche*   (Good morning, old friend arch
    t'agghie annutte lu male de   I've brought you arch
    l'arche,   disease
    E pigghiate lu male de l'arche: Take this arch disease
    buon giorno, cumpà arche.   good morning, old friend arch.)

The idea is that the illness is sent back to the constructed arches, seeing as there is no rainbow. This version from Stigliano has the same structure:

[34] *Arche sante beneditte*   (Blessed holy arch
    ngile e 'nterra stai scritte: you're written in heaven and earth:
    je passe e te salute   I pass by and greet you
    je me spoglio e tu te mute.   I undress and you are sloughed off.)

As with the method to treat a headache, the central themes of Christian myths are used as *historiolae* to treat *male dell'arco*. In Savoia, you repeat the following formula nine times at dawn and at dusk:

[35] *Sanghe fatte forte*   (Blood make yourself strong
    ca Ddie è ggiute e la morte;   because God has gone to die;
    sanghe fatte a le vene   Blood become the same as the veins
    Ca Ddie è ggiute a le pene   because God has gone to his suffering
    sanghe fatte a te   Blood become the same as yourself
    ca Ddie è ssute da le pene.   because God has come out from his
                                                          suffering.)

The regenerating story of sick blood in *male dell'arco* is marked by the rhythms of Christ's death and resurrection.

To treat scabies (*a rugna*) in Ferrandina, people use a spell that has as its central feature the *historiola* of St. Peter and Jesus:

[36] *S. Pietro da Roma venìa*   (St. Peter came from Rome
    chiaggendo e lacrimando scìa   he left wailing and shedding tears
    Acchiò o' maestro pe' via: He ran into his master:

—*Ce jé Pietro ca vai chiangendo?*	—What are you crying for, Peter?
Sta' zitte maestro mio	Be quiet, my master,
tegno la rugna e la capa pennata	I've got scabies and my head is full of scales
e da tutti so schifate.	and everyone is disgusted by me.
Pigghia nu poco d'uogghie	Take a bit of oil
e nu poco di pisciate	and a bit of piss
e la tigna t'è sanate.	and the ringworm will be cured.)

You spread the mixture of oil and urine three, five, or thirteen times, according to whether the sufferer is a child, an adult, or an old man. In Ferrandina, pleurisy (*a punta a' spalla*, literally "shoulder stab") is treated by using hot oil on the shoulder and rubbing it in while reciting the following formula:

[37] *Pintura vola vola*	(Fly, fly away, stab
allontana da la spalla e 'o core:	get away from the shoulder and the heart:
pozza sta tant'anni lontana	may you remain faraway for as many years
pe' quanti pili tene lu voie	as are the hairs of an oxen.
Padre, Figliuolo e Spirito Santo.	Father, Son, and Holy Spirit.)

You repeat the formula three times in a row: morning, evening, and the next morning.

Once again in Ferrandina, the spell for treating rheumatisms utilizes the succession of days in Holy Week, closing this list with the verse "*Fermate dolore non scì cchiù innante*" (Stop, pain, don't go any further).

Sores, wounds, and burns are widely featured in popular magic in Lucania. In Ferrandina, there are several treatments: you spread the injury with lamb or kid goat grass—"virgin" animals—or else with a concoction made with beeswax (*a' citrina*), pure oil, rue oil, and virgin animal fats, or with soot from the hearth's chimney. In Viggiano, the following spell against burns can also be used against toothache:

[38] *Fuche t'arreste:*   (Fire, halt:
      come Giuda tradì nostro Signore   as Judah betrayed our Lord
      Gesù Cristo   Jesus Christ
      int'a lu giardine terrestre   in the terrestrial garden
      così o' fuche s'arresta a stu   So will this Christian's fire be
      cristiane.   halted.)

CHAPTER FOUR

Childhood and binding

The magical representation of illness is particularly concerned with childhood, which is especially exposed to the threat of binding. Here, too, the power of ritual words, gestures, or amulets serves as protection, as a ritual set within the permanence of a certain "substance."

The drama begins even before birth, during the mother's pregnancy. The newborn's destiny appears tied in a thousand ways to what his mother does during pregnancy. She must control her actions in a countless number of ways, doing some things and not doing others, all of which fall within the order of magical associations. In Grottole, mothers fear that their babies will be born with "rough" or "prickly" skin, so during pregnancy they will carefully avoid burning wild pear wood in the hearth, since it is indeed rough and prickly. Should a mother happen to do this, she will have to undo it through the same flame that generated the evil influence: she must wet the baby's swaddling clothes and leave them to dry with the wild pear's fire, so that the evil rises up and disperses together with the steam. In Grottole, Stigliano, Viggiano, Pisticci, and Valsinni, a future mother worries that her baby might be born with his umbilical cord around his neck: she will therefore be careful not to pass underneath a rope, not to cross her hands when leaning back on a church pew, and not to place a skein of yarn around her neck. Should she accidentally happen to do one of these unlucky actions she must remedy things by undoing it, for example by passing beneath the rope in the opposite direction. In Grottole, a future mother is anxious that her newborn will be afflicted with *seretedda* (little saw): an incomplete joining of the margins of the skull's longitudinal suture. For this reason, she will be careful not to pass near a carpenter when he is sawing or step in sawdust that has fallen to the floor. It appears that there is a formula for warding off the evil forces that might arise from such an occurrence, but the informants were reluctant to recite it. In Grottole, again, another risk for a pregnant woman is to drink from a small cask that is used for drawing water from the fountain: her child will be born with a mouth that is a wide as that of the little cask. In Savoia, it is dangerous for a pregnant woman to come across two dogs mating: her child will be born with a defect of the sacrum that is called "dog's paw." In Stigliano and Viggiano, if the future mother walks across the blood of a butchered animal or on water that was used to wash fish, her child will come down with *pivile*, a form of a progressive wasting disease. In Savoia, it is specifically stockfish whose water is particularly contagious in this regard. The associations that support these magical connections are evident: a dead animal drained of its blood and a fish without blood, in particular dried stockfish, are connected with a child's anemia; they are connected with the representation of a shriveled body that no longer has life nor vital humors.

Pregnancy, just as in all critical moments of human existence, is generally an organic-psychic condition of magical morbidity and of a predisposition to succumb to influences that will harm the baby. This state of magical morbidity follows the pregnant woman in all of her daily tasks. On the basis of associations that have become traditional, the future mother's worries tend in every moment to transform themselves into threatening realities, evil allusions, unlucky omens. It is interesting to note how all of the usual actions of Catholic devotion—for example, prayer in church before an image of the Madonna—are not free from risk: in Valsinni, the future mother must murmur, "Beautiful like you, but of flesh and blood like me,"[1] and in Stigliano, "Beautiful like you, but of flesh and blood and with speech like me." The Madonna and baby Jesus

---

1. The Italian expression is *carne e ossa* (literally "flesh and bones"), translated idiomatically here. —Trans.

are certainly a lovely image of maternity but they are not flesh and blood, they neither move nor talk: this connection to allusive images requires a rebalancing compensation.

Another set of magical preoccupations has to do with predicting the baby's sex. The aforementioned customs tend to eliminate ongoing influences: those regarding forecasts of the baby's sex remove the uncertainty on a point of special interest, given a preference for the male sex due to obvious economic reasons. In Colobraro, there are various methods for prediction: you lay a loom rod at a crossroads, and the sex of baby will depend on that of the first passerby. In Viggiano, you ask a girlfriend suddenly, "Why are your hands dirty?"; if she looks at the backs of her hands, the baby will be a boy, if she looks at her palms, it will be a girl. Again in Viggiano, a particular type of homemade pasta will be thrown into a pot of boiling water: if it moves into a vertical position, this means it will be a boy, whereas if it lies horizontally, it will be a girl, et cetera. It should be observed how the symbolism of sex is related to the conventional position during coitus (a man's back, a woman's front or palm) or the genital organs. In other prediction techniques, things in an even number symbolize a male, while an odd number symbolizes a female.

The investigation of childbirth's magical ideology yielded relatively scanty results. In Viggiano, there is a connection between the phases of the moon and how the labor will go, in the sense that the delivery will be easy if the moon is full but difficult if waning. A difficult delivery is sometimes connected with some spell that has been placed on the pregnant woman. There is also the custom of assisting the labor by undoing some stitches in the mother's slip or in the mattress on which she lies. As we will see, death is also assisted by opening stitches of the mattress on which the dying person lies, since in both cases it is necessary to assist a painful coming out, a pregnant woman's child and a dying person's spirit.

A whole other set of magical worries for the mother concerns the risks to which the baby is exposed right after birth, through childhood and beyond. The infant has a fragile, precarious existence, particularly subject to the dangers of envy and evil eye. Children struck by the evil eye cry, vomit, turn pale; they can even *scattare*—"drop dead"—from evil eye. Caution is necessary precisely when they are healthy and thriving, because they are exposed to the irrepressible pang of envy on the part of other mothers. If you go to visit a home where there are children, it is advisable to pay them an ostentatious ritual greeting upon entering: "Grow, St. Martin," meaning "grow in the name of St. Martin," the saint of abundance and strength. This greeting is paid to the children with the double aim of defending oneself from uncontrolled envious impulses, and at the same time, to reassure a mother who might harbor suspicions of this. The newborn's first bath must be done in warm water and wine, or even warm wine, with wine's tonic qualities in mind.[2] Then, immediately after dipping the child in it, the liquid gets thrown out of the home if the baby is a boy or into the hearth's ashes if it is a girl. This practice is a first determination, confirmation, or consecration of destiny, in the sense that a man will have to walk out of the house, while a woman will remain bound to the hearth. At the same time, the wine symbolically spreads over the roads of the world and makes them propitious for the man who will have to travel them, just as it makes the hearth propitious for the woman who will have to remain bound to it. The newborn's first bath takes on the significance of a wine baptism according to an image of health and fortune that is even reflected in folk literature: "*Me battezzarie a n'a fontana 'e vine/addò se battezzaie lu pape a Rome*" ("I was baptized in a fountain of wine where the pope in Rome was baptized"), and it compensates for the image of a woeful birth and a life that is unlucky from the beginning: "*Quanne nasciett'io me morse mamma,/tata me morse lu jorne venenne*" ("When I was born, mamma died/and papa died the next day"), or: "*Quanne nascett'ie mamma non c'era/era sciute a lavè l'ambassature./ La naca ca m'aveva nachè/era de ferre e non se tuculeva/lu prete ca m'aveva d'abbatescì/sapeva lesce e non sapeva scrivere*" ("When I was born mamma wasn't there, she went to wash my swaddling clothes. The crib where she cradled me was iron and didn't rock, and the priest who was supposed to baptize me knew how to read but not how to write").

Other customs feature the same theme of the newborn that needs to be magically confirmed and protected. One associates the idea of particular endurance, stability, and support to the supporting beam of the roof of the house, worn through the years but that has withstood the test of time: in this way, the head of the family is *o' trave de la casa*, which is solid despite the years: "*Mantinete forte, trave de la casa/finché 'nchiana lu*

---

2.   In Lucania and many other parts of Italy, wine is also associated with the figure of St. Martin and his feast day, November 11. —Trans.

ciuccie a la cirasa" ("Stay strong, house beam, until the donkey climbs the cherry tree"). So it is understandable that one way to strengthen a newborn in Ferrandina is to cover him with dust from the beam; or else, using the powers of fire, the baby is brought before the opening of a warm oven, and the action of placing it in the oven is mimed. In Valsinni, up until a few decades ago a nail was driven where the child was born, the spot where the mother placed a vessel on which she laid the newborn, following a means of childbirth that no longer exists. *Il chiodo ferra* ("the nail binds") meant that it nailed the child into its existence, precisely because the baby has a tenuous, fluid, and fleeting existence. In its folk interpretation, even Catholic baptism participates in the same ideological atmosphere.

In general, the manifestation of "growth" reveals a transition, a movement, a changed state: there is an accentuation of magical risk because things that are tenuous, problematically placed within existence, can be nullified (dropping dead) or not pass to the new state in the proper way. Teething, the growth of nails and hair, weaning, the first outing all therefore constitute revelatory facts of a condition that changes, of a life that moves forward in existence. Thus each of these facts reignites the magical arena, in its succession of risks, nullifications, and countermeasures of confirmation. In Colobraro, when a baby loses his first tooth, it is hidden in a hole and a spell is recited that invites a magical mouse to take the old tooth and leave one of his own, so sharp, sturdy, and functional. The first cutting of hair or nails also needs protective measures: a woman will act on behalf of a girl, and a man for a boy, beginning with ties of alliance and protection that will be complete when they become, respectively, godmother and godfather of the child. Similarly, nursing must take place for an uneven number of months of the baby's age, due to the association that links the representation of uneven numbers with change. Thus, the first dressing of the child must take place in uneven months. For the first outing, which must never take place before forty days after birth, a visit to a church serves as a protective measure, following the model of the visit to the temple paid by the Madonna and baby Jesus.

In its folk interpretation, even Catholic baptism participates in the same ideological atmosphere.[3] Owing to its exorcistic qualities, baptism

---

3. This line is repeated from above and appears in the original text. —Trans.

has an efficacy analogous to that of a wine bath or the supporting beam dust, or the nail that "binds," consolidating and strengthening the baby's fragile existence, protecting it above all from evil eye: someone "baptized" is basically someone who is immune to "binding." A charm from Colobraro reminds the evil forces that their victim has been baptized, thus magically immune because of the baptism: *Binding moving through the street, don't go to N. N. because his flesh is baptized*, as one spell goes, which we will return to below. Even when a pig has evil eye—it loses weight or does not fatten enough—it gets baptized with saltwater as a remedy. Due to the magical value of the baptism, the behavior of the baby or the godfather during the ceremony at the baptismal font takes on a symbolic value for reading or determining fate. If the baby is quiet or cries, it is a good sign, and he will have a long life. If he sleeps, he will die young. If the godfather does not repeat the priest's prayer exactly, the child will be a stutterer; and so on. A child's magical morbidity is drastically intensified when the baptism, for various reasons, does not take place right away: the various phases of growth thus become particularly risky, as evidenced for example by the belief that it is not good to perform the first nail cutting if the child has not been baptized. The extreme contagiousness of evil forces, which is the primary feature of magically "exposed" moments—ones that are insufficiently protected and guaranteed—fully impacts the unbaptized child. In Grottole there is a belief, obviously influenced by the church, which clearly reflects this ideological theme: if the mother of a child who has not yet been baptized gives her neighbor a bit of fire from her hearth, the child will fall ill with "pagan fire" (*fuche paianidde*), becoming red as a little devil, thereby displaying his pagan nature. In and of itself, giving fire from one's hearth is a "strong" action that can provoke contagion, and a child lacking sufficient magical protection will suffer the consequences right away.

In its folk interpretation, the ceremony at the baptismal font fits into an overall magical framework. However, this readaptation is not entirely successful, since canonical baptism does not completely satisfy some of the needs that belong to the magical sphere. The ceremony at the baptismal font takes place far from the *naca* [crib]; especially in its first months, the child lives in its crib, and it is here that the magical threats concentrate and there is the greatest need for protection, confirmation, and consecration. This explains how, in Ferrandina, above and beyond a canonical baptism at the baptismal font, folk tradition preserves an additional baptism at the crib. On the evening of the day in which the canonical baptism has taken place, the family places around the crib seven chairs, a basin, and a towel, and the child's layette is laid out on the crib. At midnight on the dot, seven fairies will come to bless the crib, the child, and the layette, using the purifying water from the basin and drying themselves with the towel.

In the context of this special need for the child's protection, especially during infancy and childhood, people use magical sachets called *abitini* in Lucania. These are little cloth bags, usually with a rectangular shape, associated with the amniotic membrane (the so-called shirt), of which it represents the symbolic continuation. Given the apotropaic importance that baptism has assumed among all of the forms of struggle against evil forces, people naturally feel strongly about baptizing the *abitino*, which is hung from the baby's neck during the ceremony at the baptismal font. The baptized *abitino* of the first born has particular power, and so when the child who must be baptized is not the first born, an *abitino* from a first born is hung on his neck; in this way, even the children who were not lucky enough to be first born can obtain particularly effective *abitini* by proxy. The contents of the magical sachets vary: a piece of a horseshoe from a horse that has been "shoed" for the first time, three grains of wheat, three grains of salt, a hair from a black dog, a ribbon from "a priest's stole," images of saints; three grains of wheat, three of salt, three of pepper, three straw crosses, a few saints' images [*santini*]; a number of grains of wheat, fox teeth (especially during teething), pieces of communion wafer, an unmeasured ribbon, some pinches of salt purchased at different tobacconists, crossed pins placed on a piece of cloth, a piece of bell rope, some saints' images; a pinch of ashes, three grains of wheat, a bit of salt, a bit of wheat bran, two pins tied in a cross, a few saints' images; et cetera. As already noted, the *abitini* are either tied around the child's neck, or they are fastened to his personal garments with a pin. In Tricarico there is the custom of hiding a pair of scissors with the pointed ends facing up in the swaddling clothes.

Once assembled, the contents of the *abitini* are not definitively set, but they may receive additions with an eye to various critical moments in childhood. For example, during the period of teething, one may add fox teeth. In the past, the *abitini* were not worn only as infants and toddlers, but instead stayed with a person throughout his life: today, of course, this is a custom that is going by the wayside. It is nonetheless explicitly attested to in Colobraro that even an adult must not abandon his *abitino*, or at least he must wear it again in important moments of his life, for example when he goes to fairs to make purchases. In general the items in the magical sachets are always determined by specific traditional associations, blended together with themes of pagan-Catholic syncretism. Thus, for instance, there is a clear connection between a "ribbon" and the possibility of "tying up" the spell and blocking it through the magic of the knot. That the ribbon must be "unmeasured" simply means that it must not be a ribbon used for profane purposes: the "sacred" quality of this sui generis ribbon is expressed precisely in the fact that when one goes to the notions shop, he must ask the shopkeeper to cut a piece at random, "unmeasured." Similarly, the scissors pointing upward threaten to "cut"—and thereby interrupt—the forces of evil: they therefore represent a magical weapon positioned for action. Other amulets (for example, the piece of string from a priest's stole) partake in the magical form of sacred accouterments and things connected with the church's ceremonies. Analogously, as our informant expressly stated, the piece of bell rope has an exorcistic value due to the simple fact that the invisible evil force circulating in the air is forced to count how many times the rope has been pulled to ring the bell: this tricks it and makes it waste time, to the point that it gets discouraged and must give up on its plans. Thus the bell rope takes on the well-known traditional ideology of the broom as a means for busying the evil eye with counting the broomcorn strands making up its brush, keeping it at bay through this trick. In other instances, old and new explanations coexist, as in the case of pins, which originally must have been associated with the basic idea of pricking the bearer of spells and enchantments. Today, alongside this explanation, there is a second one according to which the binding, when it comes upon a cross made of pins, is unable to decide if it is Christ or the devil: the cross reminds him of Christ, the pins of the devil. Plagued with doubt, and itself bound by the contradiction, the "magic" gets ensnared and eventually gives up its endeavor.

As we have observed with regard to the baptism of the seven fairies, the magical protection of the child, especially in the first months of life, is centered on the crib. The *abitino* with its amulets is not sufficient:

specific amulets are necessary for the crib: a twig of savin, a key, a small dagger, two pieces of iron in a cross. Despite the lack of direct documentation from Lucania, we should not rule out that the knot tying the crib's rope was at one time counted as a magical knot, protective against malignant forces, evil eye, spirits, and the like. Formally, lullabies appear to be full of Catholic elements: the Holy Family and the saints, especially the Madonna, commonly appear in them, both to help the mother to enchant sleep and to ensure effectiveness of the frequently auspicious contents of the various couplets. Nonetheless, aside from the enchantment of sleep that clearly demonstrates the magical moment of lullabies, what takes place here is also a passionate enchantment of luck, a fairy-tale transfiguration of the real situation, and an anticipation of fortunate destinies dominated by the theme of wealth and power.

Children's magical vulnerability forms an important domain within the framework of "maternal magic"—customs connected with mothers' concern for the particular existential fragility of their children. Besides being a part of recurrent illnesses and ailments in this context, symptoms that strike the imagination more for their strange, astonishing, mysterious, highly visible quality, and for the discomfort to which they give rise in both the child and his mother, fall within the sphere of "magical children's illnesses." In Grottole, to "cut" children's worms, the healer opens the practice by tracing a cross on the child's stomach, pushing her thumb against the navel, and pronouncing the well-known rising and falling spell of the Holy Week:

[39]   Holy Monday, Holy Tuesday, . . . Holy Sunday
       St. Catherine, cut —'s worms
       Holy Sunday, Holy Saturday, . . . Holy Monday
       St. Catherine, cut —'s worms.

The rising and falling series and the appeals to St. Catherine are repeated three times in a row. The technique of this spell is clear: through words, the Holy Week is first laid on the child's stomach, then removed, thus operating like a poultice spread on the zone, absorbing and taking evil away, and then leaving the afflicted area. In Ferrandina, one scratches off a bit of soot of three rings from the *camastra* (the chain of the hearth to which the cauldron is suspended) and places it in water; the potion is

filtered and given to the sick child to drink. The tonic effect of iron from
the *camastra*, the sacredness of the domestic hearth, the virtuous proper-
ties of the fire from which the soot comes, and the ability of dirt (from
the "blackness") to absorb the "dirt" of the organism—recall the dirty rag
in the treatment of breast engorgement—all seem to be magical associations underlying this custom.

The unjoined edges of the longitudinal suture of the skull—known
in dialect as *seretedda* (little saw)—are a source of worry for the mother
from her pregnancy on. If, despite all of the magical precautions observed during this period, the child suffers from *seretedda*, folk medicine
will come to his aid with other remedies. In Pisticci, the healer treats
the child suffering from *seretedda* by tracing a cross on his head, tying an
unmeasured red ribbon around his head, and accompanying the operation with this formula:

[40] On you I place this ribbon
         with my left hand:
         on you, innocent child.

This is followed up with an Our Father and an Ave Maria. The child
must keep the ribbon around his head for thirteen days, and each day
the spell is repeated, moving the knot slightly. In Colobraro, the same
condition is treated by putting on a cap bonnet that has previously been
exposed to incense fumes: the cap bonnet is not removed until the condition is healed.

Another recurrent affliction that receives magical treatment is sublingual cyst. Touching the cyst with a male key[4] is the most frequent way to
enchant it: but the formulas and other particularities of the practice vary
from town to town. In Pisticci, people trace a cross on the child's tongue
and mouth, and recite the following spell:

[41] *Ti vi pi esse zer*[5]
         Ti vi pi esse zer

---

4.   In Italian *chiave mascolina*, a type of key without a hole at the end. —Trans.
5.   The "i" is pronounced as a long "e" sound in English; these are the letters of
      the alphabet "t," "v," "p," "s," and in a dialect form, "z." —Trans.

This is followed by three signs of the cross, an Our Father, and an Ave Maria. Then, the spell is repeated once again ending with three signs of the cross, an Our Father, and an Ave. The letters of the alphabet are among the last (it should not be ruled out that the original formula maintained the alphabetical order: *pi-esse-ti-vi-zer*): and this repetition of the terminating sequence would magically introduce the end of the evil condition holding the child prisoner. Another formula from Tricarico for enchanting the cyst (*rànele*) belongs to the type of spell featuring a *historiola*:

[42] *Sope 'nu tempetille*   (On a little mountain peak
      c'era quattro voiarille: there were four little oxen
      'a cap'e rànule 'a scazzavane. that crushed the head of a frog.
      Fucitinne ranele de la vocca: *Rànele*, leave the mouth:
      La chiave de la Chiesia non si The church key must not be
      tocca.   touched.)

In the process of reciting this, one makes signs of the cross with a male key before the child's mouth. In order to understand the last verse of the version from Tricarico, one must know that in the past, old wives stole the church key because it was particularly effective in treating *rànele*. The local clergy had to intervene with exhortations, orders, and threats to put an end to the violation. Memory of this is preserved in the spell, which repeats the prohibition (the church key must not be touched!), and at the same time—probably—utilizes the magical efficacy that comes from citing this powerful key, which is coveted but not allowed. The use of the key in the practice that accompanies the spell is missing in some villages and it is instead substituted by other things. For example, in Colobraro *sciscia* (the local name for sublingual cysts) is treated by placing a bit of honey and salt on the child's mouth and reciting the spell of the mound:

[43] *Sopa 'nu cuzzagnelle*   (On top of a mound
      so tre galantomme   there are three gentlemen
      ch'aràvane e sevaràvene   who plowed and plowed
      e cacciavane l'uocchie a la raune. and crushed the frog's eyes.)

If the infant is a girl, the three gentlemen are substituted with three *signurelle* (young women, girls). The formula is recited for three evenings in a row before sundown. Once again in Colobraro, there is a type of nursing cyst called *funge* (fungus), which is treated with nothing less than a cat's tail and a formula that goes as follows:

[44] *Fuie, fuie latte*   (Run away, run away milk
          ca t'arrive la coda d'a' gatta.   'cause the cat's tail is getting you.)

To enchant *pívele* (when an infant loses weight, is palid and weak), a mother pays calls on as many neighborhood women as the baby's age in months, asking each for a glass of water in which pasta has been cooked and three pinches of salt, without divulging the use she will make of them. If the women are indiscrete and want to know, she must give an evasive reply. Once home, the mother prepares a bath with the collected water and salt and places the infant in it. In Viggiano, the bath must take place in water that has been mixed with vino cotto[6] after the following spell has been recited:

[45] *Domine Ddie*   (Lord God,
          Lièvale su pivule   remove this skinniness
          a ssu figghie mie.   from my son.)

During the bath, the mother massages the sick baby's body, working from the right side to the left. There is a special time for the success of this ritual: sundown. In Viggiano, three days before the new moon, a mother undresses her child and touches his joints, wetting her hand from time to time in vino cotto. This practice, which is preceded by three signs of the cross on the child's mouth, is accompanied by a triple repetition of the following spell:

[46] *Pívele attasse:*   (Skinniness, halt:
          ti trove magre   I find you skinny
          e ti lascio grasse!   and I leave you fat!)

---

6. *Vino cotto* or *vincotto*, as it is known in Lucania, is a sweet reduction of grape must. —Trans.

The practice is carried out the day of the new moon by bathing the child in water that has been used for cooking pasta and subsequently washing his clothes in the same water. One must take care, however, that once the operation has been conducted, the water is thrown away where the mother does not pass, otherwise she may inadvertently reabsorb the contagion and pass it on to her child.

Chapter Five

Binding and mother's milk

The birth of a baby ushers in another important series of magical events related to the risks faced by the new mother and child. Just after giving birth, the new mother takes sun in order to restore her strength. The cycle of magical representations linked to the sun (this subject will be dealt with below) allows us to suppose that, at least originally, that act must have been conceived as a restorative in a magical sense. The greatest risks, and therefore the ones most widely represented in the traditional ideology, regard nursing. In Lucania, there is a widely documented relationship between the placenta and milk. In Savoia, a woman dips the placenta is several times in a river, accompanying the gesture with this formula:

[47] *come se jegne sta borza*   (Just as this bag gets filled with
      d'acqua   water
      cussí se pozzano anghí sti menne so may these breasts be filled with
      de latte.   milk.)

She repeats the formula three times and finishes with an Our Father. In Pisticci, a stone holds down the umbilical cord and placenta in the middle of a stream, so that the water flows over them at length and the placenta gets filled with it. In Viggiano and in Valsinni, to reinforce the magical operation, a small piece detached from the placenta left in the stream may be used to prepare a broth for the mother. Once the first milk's flow is favored in this way, a host of other risks arise in connection with its loss. Because of the extreme importance of mother's milk in a setting in which its lack means wasting away, illness, and death for the infant, full breasts are a natural object of envy on the part of the other mothers, and this envious glance can steal the milk and dry the breasts up. This is a more or less intentional evil eye in one of its typical forms. Mothers therefore guard over the fullness of their breasts and protect them from the envious charge in the air that, on traditionally established occasions, threatens to steal their milk. Milk theft appears with a number of nuances, ranging from the involuntary effects of certain acts to the unintentional and unconscious envious glance, to an out-and-out conspiracy that has been intentionally plotted. In Grottole, when a woman pays a visit to a new mother, she must not leave the visited home with her own child at her breast, because she would take away the new mother's milk. The latter, alarmed, calls her friend and tells her calmly and firmly: "Please give me the milk you've taken away." To make amends, the milk thief may undo the action that created this effect by entering the new mother's house with her child at her breast. In many cases the visitor appears to be irresistibly envious of the new mother's milk. It is as if every one of her actions were basically suspicious: all it takes is a particular association, established by tradition, to turn the suspicion into a certainty. In Colobraro, if a visitor takes the new mother's child in her arms and then hands it back to the mother, brushing against her breast, this light brushing is enough to dry up the latter's breasts. Also in Colobraro, if a newborn vomits milk on the floor and a visitor inadvertently steps in it, the action of stepping automatically becomes a jealous disdain, an envy that steals. Once more in Colobraro, a visitor cannot wipe her handkerchief on a child's mouth if it is dirty with milk because there is a risk that it will dry up the mother's milk, and similarly, a woman who nurses will never be entrusted with the placenta to carry out the operation described above, otherwise it will not have the desired effect.

The generically envious disposition toward other mothers' milk can become an outright magical conspiracy that has been deliberately plotted. In Valsinni, a mother who complains of having little milk hides a pinch of salt in her baby's swaddling clothes and then asks a friend to carry the child to pay a visit to a luckier mother. Upon her return from this "magical expedition," the mother lacking milk will prepare a thin soup for herself, salting it with the salt taken from the swaddling clothes, which is thought to have absorbed the victim's milk. Having performed this ritual, the milk flows abundantly in the thief's breasts. If the victim of the theft finds out who the perpetrator was, she calls for her and asks her to make amends. The two women bear their breasts to each other and squirt out a bit of milk, while the victim says: "I don't want any of yours, and I don't want to give you mine." With this resolute expression of magical-juridical will, the spell is undone.

The envious glance dries up breasts even when the psychic drive it bears is of an erotic nature. According to what an informant from Savoia told us, thirty or so years ago it happened that a man took away a woman's milk simply because he had desired her breasts. Here is a paraphrase of the narrative: A reaper was once returning from Apulia at the end of the harvest season, and "step-by-step" ['ntappa 'ntappa], he headed on foot toward his native Potenza. During the trip he passed though Vaglio one evening. At the door to a house in the village, a young wife was seated nursing her child; focused on feeding her child, she was not aware of the reaper passing by. But the reaper was well aware of her and her florid, white breasts, and he could not help envying that splendor. He continued on his way and reached Potenza, but there he felt a strong flutter in his breasts, and touching himself, he felt that they were full of milk. So he retraced his path to give the women back what he had taken: indeed, he found her in tears because she had lost her milk. With no additional explanation, the reaper executed one of the rituals that tradition has set for returning stolen milk. He began by reciting the formula:

[48] *Tenghe 'u latte tue:*   (I've got your milk:
      ramme na fedda de pane   give me a slice of bread
      mo ce dagghe nu muzzuche   I bite into it now
      e tue m 'u scippe dicenne: And you snatch it from me saying,
      "Ramme 'u pane mio."   "Give me my bread.")

While this formula was recited, the corresponding actions were carried out: the woman silently gave the reaper a piece of bread, the reaper bit it, and the woman tore it from his mouth, repeating "give me my bread."

Having carried out this ceremony, the two separated without any additional words, and the reaper returned to Potenza, with his breasts freed from the milk, while the young woman's breasts became turgid once again.

A female dog or cat can exert milk envy in the period in which they are nursing: even between a woman and an animal there is the possibility of magical exchanges and contagion. It does not seem, however, that it is possible in this case to carry out theft through the envious glance, but only through other forms of magical relations. For example, if an animal happens to eat in a woman's dish, it will steal her milk. In order to get it back, the woman prepares a mush, has the animal eat a bit of it, and then she will eat it herself, murmuring the formula: "Give me back the milk you've stolen." The contagious relationship can also take place through the remains of a meal, for example through bones.

Aside from these "thefts" of milk and the countermeasures for getting it back, there are specific spells to obtain milk when a woman does not have it or to regain it when she has lost it. Here is one formula recorded in Savoia:

[49]	*Cala cala latte*	(Get down get down milk
	na secchia e nu piatte	a bucket and a plate
	na secchia e nu varrile:	a bucket and a barrel:
	Cala cala S. Martine.	Get down get down St. Martin.)

During the recitation, the woman grasps a nipple with a dirty rag, taking care to carry out movements that reproduce the sign of the cross. To conclude, she recites three Our Fathers, three Ave Marias, and three Glorias to St. Francis. The gestures that accompany the recitation and the Catholic elements framing it vary to a relatively large degree: the same formula, according to another informant from Savoia, does not entail the use of a "very dirty" rag, but a triple sign of the cross with a thumb brushing the nipple. Moreover, according to the same informant, the formula must be repeated three times, beginning with an "In the name of the Father" for each time and after completing the entire operation, reciting ten Glorias, ten Ave Marias, and ten Acts of Sorrow. A spell from Colobraro uses the members of the Holy Family as operating forces:

[50] *In nome di Gesú e di Maria*   (In the name of Jesus and Mary,
        'u latte se n'è gghiute via;   the milk went away;
        In nome di Gesú e di Giuseppe In the name of Jesus and Joseph
        'u latte venisse 'npiette.   so that the milk comes to the breast.)

Jesus and Maria are negative operating forces, while Jesus and Joseph are
the positive magical countermeasure: the need for assonance and to identify who is responsible for the charm and who is capable of undoing it are
the criteria here of fundamental distribution of the three principal members of the Holy Family in the two opposing camps of magical struggle.

In connection with nursing, the sphere of magic also deals with breast
engorgement, which in dialect is called *o' pile a' menna* (hair in the breast),
because a hair is assumed to have obstructed the milk duct. Women treat
this condition—which happens frequently during nursing—with a spell
that is very common. Here is a version from Grottole:

[51] *Bona sera Maria du Quarmine!*   (Good evening, Mary of Carmel;
        O' quatacomere s'acchio passando. The dwarf happened to pass by.
        Chiere gente ca 'o vederne,   The people who see him
        se metterne tutte a rire.   can't stop laughing.
        —Vu ca derite a sederite sopa   —On you all who laugh and
        de me   snicker at me
        viegghie cadé nu pile d'a barba   may a hair from my beard
        mia   fall,
        viegghie scí sopa a menna vostra   may it land on your breast
        non viegghie dà o' llatte   and may you no longer have milk
        abbnanzie   to fill your children.
        —Non rerime e sederimen   —We aren't laughing and
        sopra de te,   snickering at you,
        rerime e sederime sopra di nú!   We're laughing and snickering at
                                             ourselves!

        —E già che non rerite e sederite   —Well, if you're not laughing
        sopra di me,   and snickering at me,
        viegghie calà 'o llate abbnanzie   may your milk flow abundantly
        a le file voste!   for your children!)

The spell contains a *historiola*, a mythical model of doing and undo-ing the spell, which carried out in the ritual recitation returns to oper-ate just like "that time." The *quatacomero* is a sort of bearded, deformed dwarf who is so ridiculous he moves a group of women to laugh irresist-ibly when they see him pass. Offended, the dwarf takes revenge by magi-cally making a hair from his beard pass into the women's breasts, with immediate results. The women, struck by a pain in their breasts, reassure the dwarf that they were not making fun of him, but of themselves. Once appeased, the dwarf carries out the inverse operation, taking back the hair from his beard and freeing the women of the engorgement.

The *quatacomero* of the version from Grottole becomes in Colobraro "an old, old man, more beard than person":

[52] *Passaie pe' 'na funtana*   (I passed by a fountain
      tre zitelle ca lavavene   where three girls were washing
      passaie nu vecchio vecchione, an old, old man passed by,
      cchiú varva ca persone.   more beard than person.)

In Tricarico, the *historiola* instead speaks of a certain Fra Trizzano, mal-formed and ridiculous, who instead of making a hair fall from his beard makes it fall from the hairdos of the women who are making fun of him:

[53] *Scietti all'acqua e la Fontana* (I went to the fountain
      acchiaie a Fra Trizzano: and I found Fra Trizzano:
      tre palme di musse e tre de cape. three palms of snout and three of
                               head.[1]

      —Vu rerite e sererite?   —Are you laughing and snicker-
                                ing?

      Jabbe de me ve ne facite   are you making fun of me?
      Adda cadé nu pile ra int'a le   A hair is going to fall from
      trizze adda scí a le zizze   your braids and go into your tits.
      ....

      —Adda 'nchianà nu pile da   —A hair must arise from your

---

1. A typographical error in de Martino's text reads "one" of head, but the original spelling reads "three," as documented in de Martino's fieldnotes (published in de Martino 1995a: 311). —Trans.

int'a le zizze	breasts
e n'adda scí int'a le trizze.	and go into your braids.)

In a version recorded in Pisticci, the magical practitioner is Saint Servino:

[54] *Santo Servino sceva camminande*	(Saint Servino was walking along
e truvaie tre donne pe' nnante.	and ran into three women
ca redevano e straredevano.	who laughed and snickered.
—Pecché donne ca rerite?	—Why are your laughing, women?
Jabbe de la barbella ve ne facite?	Are you making fun of my little beard?
Se jabbe de la barbella ve ne facite	If you're making fun of my little beard
leve nu pile de la mia barbell	I'll pluck a hair from my beard
pozza vení a la vostra mennella,	so it may enter your breast,
fredde e freve ve pozza pigghià	may you catch cold and fever
e li vostre figghie non li. pozz'allatà	and may your children be unable to nurse.
—Ué, zi vecchie, ué zi vecchie,	—Hey, old man, hey old man,
mi dole, mi dole la menna!	it hurts, my breast is hurting!
—Jabbe de la barbella ve ne facite?	—Are you making fun of my little beard?
—Grornò!	—No, sir!
—Mentre ca non site fate jabbe de la mia barbella,	—Since you aren't making fun of my little beard,
leve lu pile de la vosta mennella	I'll take the hair out of your breast
fredde e freve ve pozza passà	may your cold and fever pass
e lu figghie voste lu pozz'allattà.	and may your child be able to nurse.)

In a version from Campomaggiore, the magical practitioner is Saint Marciano. Finally, Jesus himself appears as the protagonist in another version from Pisticci, and the *historiola* is located in a holy legend that narrates how Jesus once went traveling about incognito, when he was caught in the rain and had to take cover in the home of a woman whom he asked for hospitality. Seeing him with his long beard, the woman thought he was not a very respectable guest and was not too courteous to him, so that poor Jesus was forced to sleep on some dried vine-shoots. Up to this point, the legend is a clear conflation with another spell against belly-aches that will be discussed below. Here, instead, Jesus is angered by the poor treatment he has received and sends a hair from his "little beard" into the "little breast" of the woman. But then, moved by compassion, he undoes the spell and takes the harmful hair back. In general, spells for breast engorgement are followed by devotional prayers, repeated several times, and accompanied by signs of the cross on the nipple. The same idea of a hair obstructing the milk duct is behind the practice of pass-ing a fine-tooth comb on the nipple of the sufferer. Another means of magical therapy is the use of a cabbage leaf heated by a flame. If only one breast is afflicted, in order to avoid spreading the engorgement to the other, the mother will nurse her child placing his back to the sick breast.

CHAPTER SIX

Storms

Magical practices associated with peasant labor and work in the fields have nowadays almost entirely disappeared in Lucania. It is quite natural that precisely in the sphere in which the relationship with nature is best controlled with realistically-oriented agricultural techniques, magical techniques have been destined to vanish more rapidly than elsewhere. Nonetheless, the great negative possibility for a peasant's work is a storm that destroys what has been sown: in this regard, people remember magical spells still used in Lucania in a recent or very recent past. In his book on folklore from the province of Potenza, Riviello mentions the art of commanding [*precettare*] the weather to undo an approaching storm that threatens the harvest, and the discussion here will simply add some more data. The old archpriest of Viggiano, Don Pellettieri, kindly told us that at the beginning of the century there was an old peasant who lived in Marsico Nuovo whose nickname was Pié di Porco (Pig's Foot), who knew and in all likelihood still practiced the spell to recite against storms. The spell opens with a rote formula originally developed by some parish priest or monk to help the common people with learning the rudiments of catechism and biblical history:

[55] *Uno: lu Die lu monde mantene;*   (One: God keeps the world going
  ruie: lu sole e la luna;   two: the sun and the moon;

tre: le tre patriarche	three: the three patriarchs
Abramo, Isacco e Giacobbe;	Abraham, Isaac, and Jacob;
quattro: le quattre evengeliste	four: the four evangelists
Matteo, Marco, Luca e Giovanni	Matthew, Mark, Luke, and John
cantère 'o vangele dinnanzi a	sang the Gospel in front of
Criste.	Christ.
E tu nuvola brutta oscura	And you, ugly, obscure cloud
ca sé venut'à ffa?	why have you come?
Ristuccia ristuccià.	Ristuccia ristuccià[1] [Crossing the fields].
No! Vattenne a quelle parte oscure	No! Go away to your obscure places
addò non canta lu gadde	where the cock doesn't crow
non vegeta ciampa de cavadde!	and there are no horse hoof prints.)

After this solemn opening, a sickle was used to draw a magic circle on the ground, and after the sickle was raised high in the direction of the approaching storm cloud, the actual spell was recited.

Once again, the opening follows: "One: God keeps the world going, et cetera," and the injunction "*Cale, cale, cale! Caale!!!*" (Fall, fall, fall! Faaaaall!!!") The last "fall!" was pronounced with a choleric, vibrant voice, intentionally and threateningly prolonging the *a*: the one who was supposed to "come down" from the rain cloud was the presumed evil spirit that drove it, and that now, after the recitation of such a powerful spell, would ruinously fall to the feet of the practitioner, precisely inside the magic circle traced with the sickle. In the past, the clergy used the magical theme of the evil spirits that provoke and guide the storm. Riviello himself recalls how in Potenza and the surrounding area, it was once believed that in order to force reluctant peasants to pay their necessary tithes to the monastery, certain monks led the populace to believe that they had a magic formula to hover in the air and become pilots of storm clouds so as to unleash them on the fields and destroy the harvest. The formula was, "*monaco saglie, monaco scinne, monaco*

---

1. "Ristuccia" is a dialect term for wheat stubble. This expression refers to taking a shortcut across the fields. —Trans.

saglie, monaco scinne" ("monk go up, monk go down, monk go up, monk go down"). And so it happened that, first a bit rising and then a bit falling in the air and flitting like fledgling birds, in the end these monks managed through the efficacy of their formula to become the masters of rising and falling in the air, and they flew through the skies to carry out their vendetta. It is of course hardly necessary to point out that among primitive peoples and in the ancient world we find widespread beliefs in storm spirits and deities and in magical practices to get the best of them, just as in Christian times storms were considered to be diabolical manifestations. With regard to "storm-making" monks and parish priests, Don Pellettieri told us that some thirty years ago there was a parish priest named Don Rafele who lived in Marsico Vetere, who had led the peasants to believe that he was able to fly in storm clouds and to direct them on the sown ground. Despite his venerable age, this Don Rafele had the habit of performing some exercises in the morning, perhaps to keep himself agile and nimble in serving the Lord. This was rudimentary exercise, as a parish priest in the Italian South could do thirty years ago: a few knee bends, thrusts of his arms up and in front of him, and at most a sort of vaulting performed by holding onto the back of two chairs that served as parallel bars. One morning a storm broke out with hail and wind, and even on that day Don Rafele did not want to give up his morning exercise: while it poured, hailed, and thundered outside, the good priest tried to vault between two chairs, holding himself up as best he could with the backs of the chairs. Precisely while he was doing this vaulting, he was seen from a window by a peasant woman, to whom the traditional "monk up, monk down" verse must have come to mind, as did the sinister power that Don Rafele had bragged about on other occasions. Having witnessed this scene, the peasant woman immediately ran through the town, going from door to door giving the alarm. The result was that not long afterward a crowd of peasants thronged in front of Don Rafele's house, and one can easily imagine their intentions. Don Rafele was terribly frightened by this event, and from then on—Don Pellettieri told us amusedly—he took precautions, and every time the weather looked like it was turning bad, he would go out and walk through the town, smiling amiably at his parishioners as if to say, "Here, look, I'm among you, I don't have anything to do with the disaster."

We find confirmation of the ideology of the "flying clergymen" in storm clouds in the narrative of a decrepit informant from Viggiano, ninety-five-year-old Margherita d'Armento, nicknamed "pezze i' case" ("piece of cacio cheese") because for some thirty years of her long life she nursed other people's children. Margherita recounted that once a priest attempted to seduce a widowed niece, but he was firmly refused. As a vendetta, he went to the river and began to hit the water's surface with a ladle, in the end transforming himself into a storm cloud headed to the widow's fields. Every year, on the eve of the harvest, the implacable priest repeated his magical scheme, to the great desperation of the honest widow, who saw her harvests go to ruin. One year, during the reaping of the wheat, the peasants saw a storm cloud heading their way, which was none other than the usual transformed priest. Fortunately, among the peasants that time there was a "weather commander," who recited the formula: "Holy Monday, Holy Tuesday ... Holy Saturday, Sunday is Easter and you fall down, and if you don't fall, go away river, farther away, or to the mountain." This formula is a combination of the well-known spell for worms and the theme of going and relieving oneself in solitary places, which is traditional in spells against storms: in magic's technical coherence, it was sufficient to have a common desired final outcome—to make someone or something fall to the ground—to justify the readaptation and contamination.

Chapter Seven

Magical life in Albano

On the road that leads from Potenza to Matera, around ten kilometers after the turn off for Tricarico, there is a minor road that branches off and descends toward the Basento Valley. Leaving behind Castelmezzano Murge on the left—bare beaches of gravel, inaccessible eagle and vulture nests—the road reaches the village of Albano. A magical life that is still intense and widespread engages the seven hundred families of this village, as attested by the quality and quantity of relevant data gathered during our twelve-day field stay from May 17–28, 1957. The series of illustrative documents obtained through ethnographic observation and tape-recorded interviews opens with Maria Adamo, also known as *La Silvestre*, a young peasant who was the victim of an episode of mother's-milk binding:

> —I've got a little boy, he's small, born on September 24. On the 26th my milk came: my breasts were full of milk, the 26th. On the morning of the 27th, I discovered that I didn't have even a little bit of milk, and I was without it for three days: Thursday, Friday, and Saturday. We didn't know what to think: someone said it was stolen, someone said one thing, another said another. Yes, because here the old folks say to us girls that because of envy milk gets stolen from someone who has a lot. I've always had plenty, and I nursed a girl for eighteen months; but for this boy, there wasn't even a drop of milk in my breasts. So I said to my mother-in-law,

"Mamma, let's call Teresina—an old lady—and let's have her do the formula [*orazione*] for '*pigliata d'occhio*' ['taken-by-the-eye']." The old lady came and did the formula and said: "My girl, this is *pigliata d'occhio*."
—What is this formula?
—She did a sign of the cross, said an Our Father, an Ave Maria, a Credo, and then said: "Two are offending you and three are defending you, the Father, the Son, and the Holy Spirit, *pigliata d'occhio* don't go any further." These were her words. Then the old lady went away. We had three people do the same formula just to see if a little milk would come back. After about an hour, I felt something moving inside my breasts, like ants. Dear Lord, I'm illiterate, I don't know if you understand. I thought it was a pimple I had above my breast, and that the dirt [pus] was coming out of the pimple. I said to my mother-in-law, "Give me a clean handkerchief, otherwise I'll dirty my whole shirt." And instead it was milk that began to flow. For three or four days I had it, but my breasts weren't full. I said, "Okay, even if it's a little, with a little sugar and water, a bit of corn tea, then in three or four months he'll eat a bit of baby pasta, a little *pane cotto* that's how we'll have to feed my son." And instead after three or four days, it went away again. Teresina told me, "They weren't joking; they've given you some serious eye." And for three months my milk played these tricks on me: I had some for a while, and then I didn't. I said to myself that my baby wasn't suckling, and so I nursed a two-and-a-half-year-old and another girl, but nothing came. The doctor was surprised, he said to me, "Signora, have you had a fever?" I said no. "Have you gotten upset with your husband?" No. "Signora, are you eating or are you fasting?" "Doctor, we're poor, but we're not fasting: I eat a bit of soup, a bit of bread every evening. "I don't know what to think," said the doctor.
— Did you go to zio Giuseppe?[1]
— Yes, I'm not hiding anything, I went. This boy, who weighed three kilos and eight hundred grams at birth, had shrunk to a kilo and a half. The doctor said, "The baby doesn't have anything." Some women told me, not one but two, three, really a lot, told me that if something had

---

1.   The terms *zio* [uncle] or *zia* [aunt] are used in this ethnographic context to denote affable respect for people somewhat older than the speaker, regardless of whether or not a real or fictive kinship relation actually exists. —Trans.

been done, there was an old man named zio Giuseppe. I had the way explained to me and I went there with the baby and my sister. It was December 6th or 7th. He's an ugly, ugly old man who makes you afraid just by looking at him, and the little house where he lives looks like it's about to fall down, it's so old. As soon as we arrived, he said, "So, what's this boy got?" "I don't know, they told me *go to zio Giuseppe*: the baby is dying from hunger, I don't have milk, we can't buy it because we buy bread.

— "It's not at all true that this boy doesn't have anything," he said. That day, it happened that I had a little milk in my breasts, and he said, "There's milk." "Sir, when I've got a little milk, one time I get fever, another time something else, another something else still, and the milk always disappears." And he said, "Don't worry, you have a great weakness in your heart." He had me undo the baby's swaddling, he took some cards like the ones used in a tavern, but with different marks: on one there's a dog, on another a flame, on another there are three hearts. He took the cards and shuffled them just like the ones in the tavern. He had me place a hand on the table and I raised the cards three times. Then he raised them and said, "There isn't anything here," three times. He took the cards, threw them on the ground and said, "This isn't a spell, but *pigliata d'occhio*, we call it *'mbasciata*: they gave you the eye before the baby's baptism, because if it had been after, there would have been the Lord's hand and the *pigliata d'occhio* couldn't have been so strong." I said, "Zio Giuseppe, you have to tell me the truth, if the baby is going to live, tell me, if he has to die, it means I'll see him die: but tell me all the same, that I won't be frightened." And he said, "There are children that have *pigliata d'occhio* in the lungs, some drop dead. Your baby has *pigliata d'occhio* in his gut. But don't take it too hard, your boy will live."

In Maria Adamo's story there is a character who will return frequently in the other narratives that follow: "zio Giuseppe." A few kilometers from Albano, at the "bridge of the Old Woman on the Basento River," a path heads into the wild landscape, and after a half an hour on foot or riding a mule, it takes you to the home of Giuseppe Calvello, who is also known by the nickname *Ferramosca*, or more familiarly, "zio Giuseppe."

He is the peasant *mago*[2] of the area, the one to whom people refer for questions regarding magic, the friend of the poor folk, as we sometimes heard his clients call him. The people of Albano also go to *maghi* and *fattucchiere* of other towns more or less in the vicinity—Tricarico, Oppido, or Genzano—but the magical life of Albano is dominated by "zio Giuseppe." His prestige resides in the figure of a man—as another client told us—"who knows the ancient science, and maybe recalls something, and now he's telling us." His behavior with people is in fact inspired by the model of someone blessed with the gift of clairvoyance, of guessing the name and condition of a client and the true reason of his visit. This model is evident in Angela D'Amico's narrative:

> I had a four-year-old child ill for six months. I even took her to get X-rays, blood, and urine tests: the X-rays didn't find anything, some spots on her lungs, not much of anything. The old women said a spell had been cast: "Go to Genzano," they said, "because there's a woman there who can prophesy." I went to Genzano, but the woman wanted 13,000 Lire, I said 10, but she said no: so I went to zio Giuseppe. As soon as I arrived, he said, "Hello! Have a seat, how may I help you?" I said, "You need to guess why my sweetheart in America doesn't write me anymore." He started to laugh: "You're not an old maid, you're the mother of six." (Yes, because I had six children, one died and five are living). "I don't want to divine for you anymore." He took his cards and put them away. Because I had said a lie, trying to fool him. Then I thought: but who told him that I'm married and have six children, maybe someone from my hometown. Then I was told that, no, these are *masciari*, people born before Jesus Christ....

As the cases of Maria Adamo and Angela D'Amico demonstrate, people turn to zio Giuseppe to undo spells, but they think that the old *masciaro*

---

2. The term *mago* [pl. *maghi*] is used locally to describe a figure that is much more similar to the "cunning man" than to our common image of a "magician" (cf. the discussion of *fattucchiera*, note 1, p. 4). It is also a synonym of *masciaro* [pl. *masciari*], which takes the feminine form *masciara* [pl. *masciare*]. The original Italian terms have been maintained in this translation. —Trans.

can also cast spells, especially in matters of the heart, so he sometimes finds himself in the embarrassing condition to have to undo a spell that he himself had performed. The craftsman Vito Dragonetti, age twenty-four, offers an illuminating narrative on this point:

I don't know if I can remember all of the details: if not, I'll go back and pick back up from where I left off. From the age of fourteen to eighteen, I was constantly visited at night by what the people in our area call *masciare*. I realized this when they entered through the keyhole and sat on my bed: at that point, I wanted to call my mother but the words were stuck in my mouth. Then, in order to keep them from touching me, I moved to the other side of the bed, and then I got my voice back and screamed. Like this, I sent them away and freed myself of them. When I turned twenty-two, I began to get a pain in the mouth of my stomach, and no doctor was able to figure out what it was. Examinations and X-rays: they never found anything. People told me: "Go get yourself divined, it might turn out to be something magical." So I went to someone who divines: "zio Giuseppe." He said that it wasn't an enchantment, but something you catch like you catch a cold: he had me take baths with water that had been boiled with *spigadosso*, an herb. So, since zio Giuseppe told me that it wasn't a spell, I thought: if it's not a spell, it's an illness. And I went to Potenza to get operated on but no one wanted to operate on me. Then I went to a hospital in Naples, and one day an old man who was in the bed next to mine asked to see my hand. He said: "You've been placed under a spell! You can hardly see it, though, it's a light thing, because eight people are performing the spell and eight are undoing it." Two days later, I received a letter from home that said this and that, we went to Potenza to get divined, and this "diviner" [*indovinata*] says that a spell's been put on you, and here in Albano we've now gone about getting it removed; when you come to Potenza, you can speak directly with the *masciara* and see what you need to do. So I went back home and I went to see the *masciara* in Potenza, who ordered me medicines, but I didn't get better. So then I went to a diviner from Genzano, who divined what I had: a spell on my shoulders and stomach. "A bit of time will pass, but you'll get better." And he gave me a lace and said, "Go to a crossroads, undo five knots tomorrow evening and six on Friday evening, and with each knot you undo you have to say this: Holy Devil/undo this/Dragonetti Vito.

Then, Saturday morning before sunrise, you have to burn the lace." He also gave me something to drink every morning. In fact, I felt better, so I went back to zio Giuseppe and said to him, "You told me it wasn't a spell, but an illness: why, if it was really a spell?" In my opinion he did it because some girl must have gone to zio Giuseppe before me in order to put a spell on me, and I ended up turning to precisely the wrong person. But I have no idea who the girl might have been.

The magical representation of illness reduces every pathological condition to *pigliata d'occhio*, or "something done" [*cosa fatta*]—that is, to binding or spells. This means that an illness is magically treatable to the extent that it involves an experience of domination, a feeling of being acted upon by an alien and malignant force. When a *mago* recognizes that "it's something done," this recognition is equivalent to a declaration of competence and an assumption of responsibility: otherwise, the case would call for a doctor. In an elective fashion, the realm of magically treatable illnesses features above all psychic afflictions that are directly connected to an experience of domination; second, the bodily symptoms that are related to such an experience; and third, some organic disease, at least to the degree that certain psychic elements play a greater or lesser role in it and to the pathological symptoms per se is added the experience of being acted upon by evil outside forces.

The importance of the experience of domination in the magical life of Albano is no doubt very significant. Young Dragonetti's mention of *masciare* who visited him at night from age fourteen to eighteen, leaving him unable to speak or move in a "bound" psychic condition, illustrates the magical ideology closely connected to the experience of domination characteristic of a nightmare and with a hallucinatory projection of a dominating form in the traditionalized figure of the *masciare*, *masciari*, or the like. A connection of this sort recurs consistently in much of the data gathered during our stay in Albano. A peasant woman named Grazia Lorenzo told of how her grandmother was always visited at night by *masciare* who played many "pranks" [*dispetti*] on her, without her being able to move or speak. Another woman, Maria Giovanna Giura, woke up at night and witnessed the following scene, she too was unable to move or speak: a *masciara* entered the room, took her baby girl out of the cradle and left her on a chair, she turned the cradle upside down on the bed and, finally, put everything back and left. It is common opinion that such night visits, which no one confuses with dreams, are expressly linked to attempts at "spells": the *masciara* visits someone to "bind" him with spells. Teresa Festa relates the following:

> I was sixteen and seven months pregnant when around one o'clock in the night I felt something pulling, pulling on the blankets. I looked and saw a woman who was leaning over me and who started to pinch my belly. "You sleep," she said, "and your child dies." I couldn't move, and I stayed like that for a while. Finally, I could move, and I heard a sound of hooves. The next day I miscarried. Everyone told me that someone had put a spell on me: what is certain is that I saw that *masciara*. On other occasions, too, the *masciare* did these pranks: but after I went to zio Giuseppe, they no longer came.

In other cases, lived experience gets complicated by a struggle between the victim and the *maciara*, and the next morning they bear the signs of it in bruises and scratches. One of the diviners of Albano, presented to us with the name "Filomena, the wife of Lorenzo from Tolve" referred that the *masciari* often torment her, tempting her to perform a spell, but they never succeed because she was born on Friday. One night she felt an icy hand scratching her leg and she showed us signs of this that were still visible. Filomena belonged to a family tormented by *masciari* and related analogous episodes dealing with her brother and her mother.

In the following, Concetta Gioffredo tells of one of the bothersome visits she had: "Yes, it was in this bed. It was around midnight and I felt my hair being pulled. I said, '*Madonna mia*, leave me be, leave me be this night.' I wanted to grab the person's hair, but it slipped out of my hands. I didn't even see if it was a woman or a man. I wasn't drunk, it's a true fact."

In this struggle between victim and *masciara*, the victim can defend himself if he manages to grab the *masciara*'s hair and hold it tight until dawn, murmuring some appropriate formulas for keeping a solid grip. This brief exemplification already demonstrates the restrictedness of the psychoanalytic reduction (Jones) of nightmares to the fulfillment of violently repressed sexual acts, as well as the related interpretation of the anguished feeling of total paralysis as a symbol of feminine self-denial during coitus. Actually, the experience of domination greatly transcends the case of sexual domination, and it should be interpreted above all as the experience of an individual presence that cannot manage to make itself present, and for this reason it flounders and externalizes in various forms both the attack and resistance to it. This does not rule out cases of amorous binding or sexual attacks as specific contents.

According to the common ideology in Albano, the *masciari* and the *masciare* have a nighttime meeting place, which they reach "riding on the backs of dogs," especially white ones. A peasant man named Vito Goffredo told us that for a period five years ago, a white dog showed up in the morning with dark marks on his back in the form of a saddle: this was the sign that he had been ridden by *masciare*. Another sign was the animal's fatigue. Giuseppe Molinari, another peasant, spoke to us of a dog that had been placed to guard a stall: every morning the dog appeared extremely tired and with marks on its back. Even the ideology of a witches' gathering in particular places is linked to the hallucinatory experiences of psychic voyages that the victim believes to have actually carried out. Canio de Grazia, a thirty-eight-year-old peasant, was kidnapped one night from his bed by a *masciara* riding a white dog and transported to the meeting place, a mountain near the forest of San Chirico. Some of the *masciare* wanted to cast him down from the mountain, but others saved him from this violence and brought him back home. They left him on the floor, where he was found in the morning. On another occasion when he was still a youth, Canio took a herd out to pasture; at dusk, however, the herd returned to town by itself. Worried, his parents went about looking for their son, and they found him at the bottom of a gorge, unconscious. One could see the depression in the ground caused by the boy falling into the gorge. When he came to, Canio related how two *masciare* had thrown him down the gorge, and one of them was wearing a blue skirt trimmed with black velvet. They brought him home and called for Giuseppe lo Spiritato [the Possessed], a *masciaro* from Tricarico, but his formulas were unsuccessful. On the basis of the boy's indications, his parents thought they had identified the *masciara* who had cast the spell, and they sent for her in order to repair her evil deed. The *masciara* came, rubbed the boy's body with a liquid, wrapped him in a blanket, and put him to bed, and the next morning the boy was "cured." Here, ideology displays a relationship with reality: the *masciare* who go around casting spells at night, or who may lay their snares during the daytime, are some-times imaginary figures, faceless, unidentifiable shadows: but sometimes they are particular people who live in the community, who seek revenge for some offense or impoliteness received, or else they act for envy's sake. In this sense, there is a traditionalized model of an event in which reality and hallucination are mixed to such a degree that it is quite difficult to reconstruct their respective roles. The model is as follows: during the day, if one slights a *masciara*, during the night he will pay the consequences. Here is Isabella Gioffredo's narrative in this regard:

—I was seventeen when it happened. A woman came to our house, I didn't know her, maybe she was a Gypsy, and she asked me for a piece of cheese. I was alone in the house and I told her that I didn't have any. This old lady left and said: "Okay, you don't want to give me any, I'll show you." When evening came and it was time for me to do my hair, I realized that my hair was all knotted like the fringe of a blanket, and the comb couldn't pass. So I called a woman, zia Rosa, who said: "You'd better cut it, my girl." And that's what I did. I placed the braids on top of the roof so that no one would take them, but when I went to take them back to show them around the village, I couldn't find them anymore.

—So was that woman a *masciara*?

—Yes, she was a *masciara*. That's how they've been called since before the birth of Our Lord. They say that when they die, these wretches—because that's what we should call them—they call for a child. You don't believe it, eh? You don't believe it? But it's true. They always call for a child, and then they want its hand so that its virtue passes to them. But if someone's got some sense, when she dies, instead of giving her a hand, you give her a stick, a broom, and then you burn it.

In cases such as these, which numerous independent narratives con-sistently repeat, it is very difficult to establish if the encounter with the *masciara* is ascribable to reality or constitutes a hallucinatory experience. In other situations, there is no doubt that the encounter or relationship is part of reality, as in the following case related by mule driver Vincenzo La Rocca:

When I was a youth, my sister received an engagement proposal from a peasant who was part of this band of hoodlums. An *ambasciatara*,[3] who was also a *masciara*, called my sister to her house and tried to persuade her to accept by showing her rings, bracelets, and other things that had been stolen. When my sister came home and I found out about this, I beat her. That night, however, the *ambasciatara* placed herself on my stomach and spoke with my mouth: my mouth spoke, and I couldn't stop it until my mother came and closed it, like you do for the dead. For a few minutes I stayed just like a dead person, and when I came to, I explained that Rosa Matera—that was the name of the *ambasciatara*—was on the mouth of my stomach, and that's why I couldn't answer.

In general, these episodes are to be interpreted psychologically as oneiric events that through real images and movements actualize a fundamental experience of domination. This actualization can take place both in an obvious way through displacements of the body, self-inflicted gestures of harm, and the like, as well as through unclear psychosomatic mechanisms linked to hysteria, like vasomotorial and trophic disorders, and certain unusual forms of the pilomotor reflex. In this way, the bruises and scratches, inextricably knotted hair and the like all constitute moments that are integrated into such visions and continue to be so after returning to normal waking consciousness. Occasionally the oneiric vision is completely obliterated, so that the only modifications that remain are the ones that the gestures (or the psychosomatic processes we have indicated) have brought into being—bruises, scratches, knotted or braided hair. Nonetheless, if due to this oblivion, these modifications cannot be directly connected to the oneiric vision, they are nonetheless taken to be signs and proof of the traditionalized models of experience: someone who, for example, wakes up in the morning with bruises has been tormented during the night by *masciare*, even if he has forgotten the images of the corresponding vision. There is yet another possibility that must be taken into account, although it is quite difficult to ascertain: the possibility of oneiric visions mimed by

---

3.   The *ambasciatara* was an intermediary for arranging marriages in traditional Southern Italian society, given that women could generally not be approached directly by a suitor. This custom fell into disuse after the 1960s. —Trans.

two people, in which for example the mother "plays" the part of the spell-binder, and her son that of the spellbound. Psychic interactions of this sort are, among other things, facilitated by the fact that several people sleep in the same room and sometimes even in the same bed.

Our research indicates that the basis of many recurrent episodes in the magical life of Albano lies in all of the following: the mimed oneiric vision (with a "character" who acts out all of the parts or with two characters), the introduction of corresponding modifications of reality, the possibility of a complete oblivion of the lived psychic experience, and the connection of the event with representations of binding, spell, *masciare*, and counterspell. In this way, the ideology of *masciari* or *masciare* who take infants out of the cradle during the night and place them in dangerous positions, where they are found in the morning with great astonishment (for example, on the window ledge or near the fireplace) certainly has its roots in this. Hostile drives that are repressed during waking hours are partially or symbolically acted upon during the night in an oneiric event that leaves traces in reality. The close connection between these oneiric events and magical ideology has been documented for the case of Donato Ferri, who at the age of two months was the object of a strange "tying," and from ages four to seven he got out of bed every night and took refuge "with his eyes shut" in the chimney:

The baby was two months old. One night we heard him crying, he was restless. In the morning I undid his swaddling and found his *populicchio* [penis] tied with length of cotton string all around it, with lots of knots. I undid the knots and threw the string into the fireplace. When he got bigger, from ages four to seven, the boy would get out of bed at night and with his eyes shut, go and stick himself in the chimney: we would hear him cry and ran to get him. We went to zio Giuseppe, who said that the boy went to the chimney because I had thrown the string in the fire. Zio Giuseppe also said that when he turned seven, he would get better all by himself, and he gave us an *abitino* for the boy. Then he went to a summer camp and it got stolen.

The episode of the "tied" penis clearly appeared to be the realization (mimed) of an oneiric event of the mother or some other member of the family; the episode of escaping to the chimney is clearly the mimed actualization of the boy's oneiric event. Both episodes are fused into the magical ideology of the "spell" and the link between the burnt string and the boy's subsequent nocturnal attraction to the place of the burning.

With regard to the oneiric events that take place, particularly worthy of note are those cases in which, come morning, the victim finds himself inexplicably tied up with ropes in bed or on the floor. We have seen how the experiences of Vito Dragonetti, Grazia Lorenzo, Maria Giovanna Giura, and Teresa Festa all explicitly refer to a psychic condition of domination, clearly distinguished from dream and perceived to be real, in which the victim can neither move nor speak and is forced to passively submit to torments on the part of the *masciare*. This condition of psychic domination entails a form of "binding" par excellence. It is precisely in reference to experiences of this sort that the magical ideology symbolizes the operation of binding or spellbinding with tying and knotting, and the operation of removing the spell with untying or undoing knots. On the level of the mimed oneiric event, the experience of domination can be externalized to express itself with an actual binding, carried out with material ropes and knots that immobilize the body. In the simplest case, the binding is in fact self-tying, which in the oneiric consciousness is completely merged in the representative contents of the consciousness itself, that is, in the violence perpetrated by the *masciari* or *masciare* who tie and knot. But, as has been said, one should not exclude the possibility of an oneiric scene experienced by two people, in the course of which some family member or acquaintance carries out repressed spell-binding intentions and the victim adjusts to the oneiric event of the other, falling into a state or more or less complete psychic subjection. If to this we add the possible oblivion of the event, which is testified to only by the fact that the victim finds himself "bound," we have the fundamental criterion for interpreting the episodes of actual binding that are recurrent in the magical life of Albano. Here, for example, is the story of Rocco Abate, an eighteen-year-old apprentice tailor:

—One morning, when I woke up, I found my feet tied like this, crossed. Seeing as for a long time I had suffered from a bit of nervousness, I thought it was because of this nervousness that this had happened. Not long after, around four or five in the morning, I found my hands tied to the headboard of the bed. A third time, the binding was complete: a rope passed several times underneath the bed and held me tight, without being able to move.

—What did you think had happened?

—I thought, who knows, I tied myself up, but then how could I have tied my hands? Ah, I forgot this: the third time, after having been untied by my mother, I still couldn't put my feet on the floor and walk. Just outside town there is a little old man, zio Giuseppe, and everyone in my family thought that if I went to him I'd be cured. So to save my life, my parents went: I couldn't move. Zio Giuseppe ordered a foot bath for eight days. The last evening I did the foot bath, and I saw that under my feet blood came out. After that, I felt okay.

—What does "zio Giuseppe" do when he's divining?

—One of the things he does when he's divining is that he puts a finger in his ear, like he's hearing what the "company" is saying to him. Maybe they're demons, I don't know. Certainly some spirit must inform him about everything.

—Do you remember any dreams you've had?

—No. Ah, four or five days ago, while I was sleeping, I dreamed that they were putting me in a coffin. There was a woman all dressed in black, with certain nails this long to nail the coffin. While they were putting me in the coffin, I couldn't speak or move.

The victim's father, who together with the mother had gone to see zio Giuseppe, had this to say when questioned separately:

—At first we found him tied up, speaking with all due respect, by his feet, but his legs were free: there was a little rope that passed over around his feet and was tied under the bed. A second time we found him with his hands tied to the headboard, and a third time he was all tied up, with the ends of the rope tied under the bed. I untied him that morning, too, but he couldn't walk. He stayed in bed for several days. We didn't know what to think: he could have tied himself up, but it's just not possible that he could have done the knots under the bed. So my wife and I went to this little old man we call "zio Giuseppe," an old man who can hardly walk, but since we knew that he was an expert in certain matters, we went to see him. He said, "Don't be frightened, bathe him with warm water, rub him with alcohol and with a little bottle of this stuff called Sloan. Don't worry: he'll get better. In seven day's time he will be walking, for sure he will be walking, he'll come himself to see me." And in fact, seven days later we brought him to "zio Giuseppe" on his own two feet. The last bath we gave him, the water turned red, and since then he began to walk. When the boy, cured, went to "zio Giuseppe," the old man said to him: "I wanted to make you walk to see if you actually could walk."

—Did you pay zio Giuseppe?

—No, you don't pay him. You might bring some gift, maybe a meal or things like that: but he doesn't ask for it. Zio Giuseppe says that he doesn't do it to make money but to help the poor people.

—Did your son sleep alone when you found him tied up in bed?

—He slept alone, but our bedroom.

In her report, the victim's mother was much briefer and concise:

—What did you think when you found the boy tied up?

—What was I supposed to think? The poor boy was humiliated. He was fine, he wasn't sick, and in the morning he was tied up. Even now he says: "How could it have happened that I wound up like that?" Then it occurred to us, like this, that there was this old man, and he could do something like people say, and we went, because the boy couldn't move. The old man had us do hot water washes for a week, and the last time the water turned red, as if a little blood had come out. Since then he's been walking and has been fine.

The nature of this documentation obviously does not permit us to decide if it is an oneiric event with one or two actors, and still less does it allow for any psychoanalytic interpretation of what has taken place. It is sufficient here to have highlighted that the simplistic hypothesis of a "practical joke" or a common nighttime "attack" to the detriment of the victim does not fit in with the data and that everything hints instead at an oneiric event with the actualization of its contents. The victim does not recall anything, nor do the family members sleeping in the same room: the only evidence is the tying in the morning. Moreover, the victim could not get out of bed, that is, the material binding is connected to an actual psychic *abasia* and *astasia*. This all clearly belongs to the same order as the mimed oneiric events, during which the *masciare* inflicts abuse and blows on the victim that are registered on the body. In the case of Rocco Abate, however, the event was forgotten and concerns the oneiric actualization in the sense of domination and "tying" that characterizes these experiences. In mystical literature, too, material tying carried out by the devil is a well-known occurrence. To avoid mentioning Maddalena della Croce, the diabolical abbess, let us recall the case of Teresa Noblet: according to her biographer, she was "tied by her braids" to the sideboards of the bed, and in a subsequent episode tightly bound by a rope and left on the floor. In general, in its ideological and symbolic meaning, tying is the representation of the psychic state of domination of the spellbound victim (or person tormented by the devil) and in its material actualization belongs to the mimed oneiric occurrences that are connected to the experience of domination, whether or not these events are forgotten by the victim when he regains his normal waking consciousness.

The sense of domination that characterizes the psychic state of binding or spellbinding can take on the form of more or less complete possession on the part of a second personality that is aberrant and perverse, in stark contrast to the social and moral order. In the magical life of Albano, cases are told of people possessed by spirits and the devil, exorcised by the *masciaro* or the priest. Our documentation on this point is too spotty to serve as an indication: we prefer instead to refer to the ideology of helping spirits and to the corresponding psychic experiences that support them. These spirits are not morally aberrant, nor do they invade the individual presence, leaving it practically without margin, as does happen in cases of possession. On the contrary, they are benevolent spirits who intervene in individual or family life to caution and to warn, and they behave all in all like true household spirits, obliging and zealous. A spirit of this sort lived for five and a half years in the home of the Loguercio family. When it gave signs of itself for the first time, announcing itself with the mysterious fall of some bricks from on high, Carmela Loguercio immediately drafted a ceremony of identification and recognition. She asked: "Are you Antonio? If so, hit my knee, if not, rub my knee with the palm of your hand." A hit to the knee followed: the identification was thus made. Since then Antonio—who was a man from Albano who had recently passed away—was a member of the family, helping Carmela Loguercio and her children. Once, one of the daughters, Rosa, was harvesting and fell asleep from exhaustion.

Before she fell asleep, she asked Antonio to wake her up if the mule approached the harvested wheat to eat it. At a certain moment Antonio did indeed give her a blow with a stick, which woke her up and allowed her to rush in time to save the wheat. Another time, Antonio woke up the son Rocco just in the moment in which a cow who was supposed to be guarded was about to die strangled by the rope keeping it tied. In the house, there was a bell without a clapper placed in a niche in the wall: every so often this bell would ring, and with this sound it communicated useful news and warnings. Rocco in particular maintained a relationship with Antonio through the bell, and even the neighbors took advantage of this. Thus, in the period of the war in Africa, a woman who was about to remarry after hearing that her husband had been killed in action, was informed by the bell that her husband was actually alive and would return on a certain day. The woman decided to wait, and in fact that very day her husband came back. Antonio would even play innocent tricks, which did not cause any concern. Once while Carmela was in bed, Antonio began to move her legs, and Carmela reprimanded him, annoyed: "Leave me alone and go play jokes on the girls." Antonio then took a stick and brushed her knees amiably. Antonio went away just as he had come: his presence was no longer felt, the news ceased, and the bell without the clapper remained silent. The Loguercios were sorry about this departure, because Antonio had become a member of the family, and in the end he had entertained them: "We had so many good laughs," regretted Rocco, recalling the period of the talking bell and the amiable jokes of their household spirit.

This is the magical life of Albano, whose first point of connection is the rustic house of zio Giuseppe, at the foot of the Castelmezzano (Murge). Who this *maciaro* actually was emerges from the narratives of his clients, and the interviews with the priest and the doctor, like the direct meeting with him, did not tell us much more. Zio Giuseppe's range of activities was limited by the traditional requests of his clientele: binding and counterbinding, spells and counterspells. Cases like that of Maria Adamo (a.k.a. *La Silvestre*) whose mother's milk was stolen, or the boy Donato Ferri who escaped every night to the chimney, or Rocco Abate, who woke up in the morning tied to his bed—these all make up—together with the practices for binding and releasing in love— the elective field of his activities. Given the high child morbidity (and mortality), and the terrible health and hygiene conditions of the village, his work was even requested for treating children and adults affected by more or less serious organic illnesses. In this sphere, however, zio Giuseppe agrees to intervene only when the case is a matter of "things done," that is, only when there is a psychic element of the organic illness—or one that can be artificially encouraged, and when it is possible to frame the case within an event of "doing" and "undoing" on the level of occult dominating forces and the corresponding ceremonies of "tying" and "untying." There is, too, a more obscure aspect of zio Giuseppe: his pronounced eroticism. For the most part, these peasant *maghi*, even if they are old, exercise a significant fascination on women: the famous *mago* of Valsinni, for example, lived with a young woman from Villapiana in Calabria, who was quite devoted to him. The *mago* of Albano was no exception, and a young peasant woman who lived with him was little more than age twenty. The village doctor told us that there are piquant stories that circulate about zio Giuseppe: among other things, it is said that he proposes to the peasant women to have themselves "X-rayed," which consists in reflecting their most private parts in a mirror, and many women supposedly go to have themselves "X-rayed" in this way. A young peasant woman from Bella who lived with zio Giuseppe for a period told us the following:

> Zio Giuseppe wanted to make me become a *maciara*, but I didn't want to. Zio Giuseppe became a *mago* like this: he went to the cemetery, he put money on a table and the devils told him many "words." To guess how long a woman should live, zio Giuseppe puts a card in her cleavage and then takes it back. I've heard that sometimes he puts his hand below. Another time a women had a spell, and zio Giuseppe kept her for ninety-nine days in his house, but I don't know what he did to treat her. . . .

This story, full of reticence and allusions, is not substantially different from others that we heard. But zio Giuseppe's eroticism and the erotic tie that he sometimes establishes with his clients does not contradict the figure of this peasant *mago* to whom the people entrust themselves for better or worse.

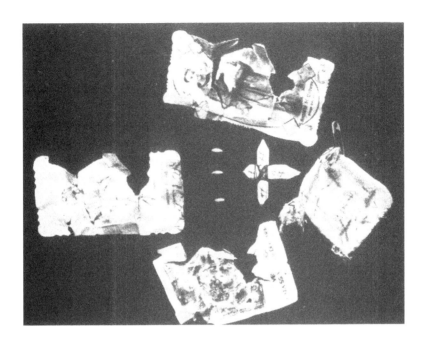

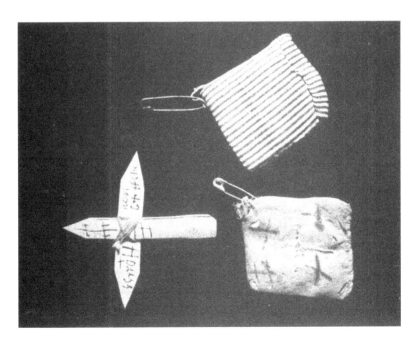

Figures 1 and 2. Equipment making up the *abitini*.

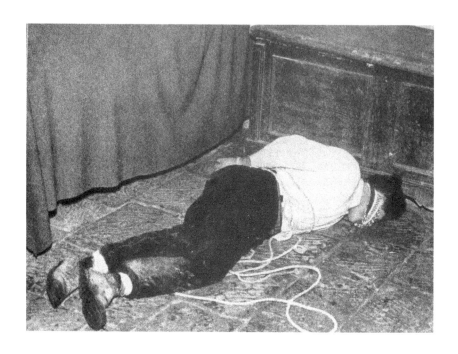

Figure 3. Reconstruction of a case of nighttime "tying."

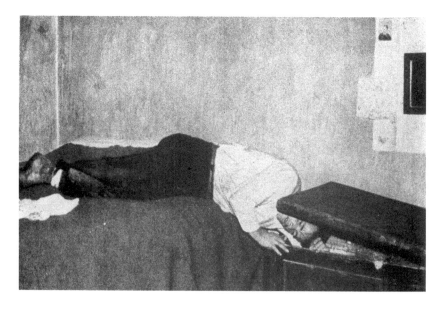

Figure 4. Reconstruction of a night "torment."

Figure 5. A plowshare beneath a bed to ward off binding: this is particularly important for a wedding night's good outcome.

Figure 6. Lamentress from Pisticci.

Figure 7. *Fattucchiera* from Colobraro.

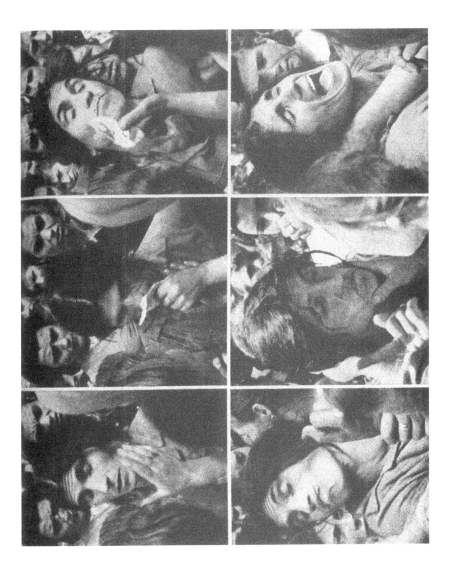

Figure 8. During the festival of Saint Bruno (Serra San Bruno, Calabria) a women enters into a state of possession. An unsuccessful attempt to exorcise her is made by having her kiss an image of Saint Bruno. Despite a second attempt at exorcism, the aberrant and perverse personality that has taken control of the woman does not let go of her.

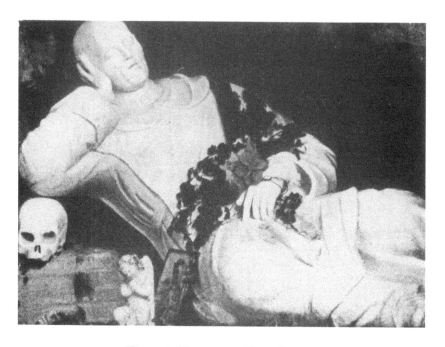

Figure 9. The statue of Saint Bruno.

Figure 10. Public confession of sins: the festival of the Madonna del Belvedere in Oppido Lucano.

Figure 11. Procession to the Madonna of Pierno.

Figure 12. Montemurro: an *ex voto* to Saint Rocco.

Figure 13. In the chapel of Saint Paul in Galatina, a *tarantolata* has been jumping for a few hours on the cornice of the altar.

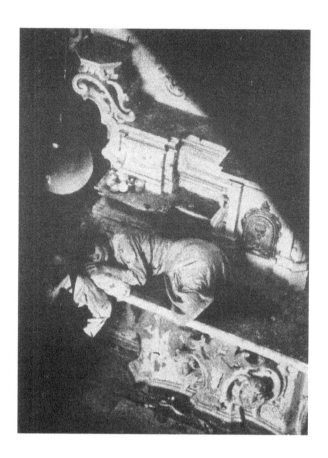

Figure 14. After a period of rest she resumes her jumping dance.

PART TWO

Magic, Catholicism, and High Culture

Chapter Eight

The crisis of presence and magical protection

If we ask why such an archaic ideology still survives in present-day Lucania, the most immediate reply is that despite modern civilization, even today an archaic regime of existence involves a broad segment of social strata in Lucania. A number of conditions certainly favor the maintenance of magical practices: the precariousness of life's elementary goods, the uncertainty of prospects for the future, the pressure exercised on individuals by uncontrollable natural and social forces, the dearth of forms of social assistance, the harshness of toil in a backward agricultural economy, and the limited memory of rational, efficacious actions with which to realistically face the critical moments of existence. One might say that the root of Lucanian magic, as with any other form of magic, is the immense power of the negative throughout an individual's lifetime, with its trail of traumas, checks, frustrations, and the corresponding restrictedness and fragility of the positive par excellence of realistically-oriented action in a society that "must" be made by man and reserved for man, faced with a nature that "must" ceaselessly be humanized by the demiurgic work of culture. Even so, this relationship between the existential regime and magic remains generic and obvious, and fundamentally rather inconclusive. The themes of magical power, binding, possession, spells, and exorcism are undoubtedly connected to the immense power of everyday negativity that menaces individuals from the cradle to the grave, but the nature of this connection remains vague. Analogously, magical ideologies regarding pregnancy, delivery, nursing, weaning, and the risks an infant faces in his early years are all without a doubt related to the data regarding the high number of pregnancies and miscarriages, stillbirths, problems with nursing, to the lack of forms of assistance for women during pregnancy and childbirth, for mothers and children;[1] we might also appeal to ignorance, illiteracy, and so forth. With this, however, we would not go much further than an "enlightenment" or "positivist" type of approach in which magic is in any case mixed up with the aberrations of the human mind, or even with the deliria dealt with in psychopathology. The analytical discourse becomes more conclusive when we attempt to trace the psychological meaning of what we have pointed to as the power of the negative in the Lucanian existential regime. Now, this psychological meaning sheds light on a much more serious negativity than any lack whatsoever of particular goods: it sheds light on the risk that

---

1. In a report by hygienist Mario Pitzurra published by the Istituto di Igiene of the University of Perugia, we read the following data for Albano di Lucania: "Here, children are born and die in an uninterrupted wave, one that neither fills nor leaves gaps, in a cycle of existence reduced to the pure vegetative life. The mother of the family has many pregnancies: ten to fifteen. Some of these end up in abortions—miscarriages, of course. The others reach their conclusion: seven, ten, thirteen children born. Of these births, many die within the first years of life (C. P., a 37-year-old woman, has given birth to twelve children and has had two miscarriages: seven of her children died by age four.) Stillbirth rates are very high: out of 66 births in 1956, there were four stillbirths (6%); out of eighteen births up to May, 1957, there were six stillbirths (16%). In children who survive beyond their first year, the environment affects their psychic and physical development quite seriously: this fact can be garnered by even the most superficial examination of the population of children. One constantly observes children with problems in walking, teething, and speech, with serious alterations of the growth curve, with consistent notes of rickets, with serious signs of encephalitic pathologies (microcephaly, cretinism, oligophrenics). Out of 177 children in elementary school (between ages six and fourteen), only seventeen featured normal thyroids. The closest hospital (that of Potenza) is thirty-five kilometers away, and the village has no pharmacy. There are no specialized surgeries of any type whatsoever except for the surgery of the Opera Nazionale Maternità e Infanzia, which is open only on certain days of the week" (Pitzurra 1957).

the individual presence itself gets lost as a center for decision and choice, and drowns in a negation that strikes the very possibility of any cultural action at all. The relative frequency and intensity of episodes of the frailness of presence was already highlighted in the magical life of Albano: the oneiric experiences of domination externalized in witches' torments, the mimed or even psychosomatic actualization of certain hallucinatory contents, the acting out—this, too, oneiric—of impulses repressed during the state of wakefulness all already offer proof of a pronounced fragility of individual presence. But oneiric events of this sort, twilight-state impulses that interrupt the waking state, hallucinations following traditional patterns, uncontrolled crises of paroxysm or stupefying dullness in critical moments highly charged with emotion, more or less frequently mark the "magical life" of all of the Lucanian villages. An example of a haircut carried out by a girl in a momentary twilight state, followed by total amnesia, was documented in the following narrative of A. R., former mayor of Castelsaraceno:

> I was the one who was called, back then I was mayor. One morning the girl's mother came and said to me: "Come over to my house, because this and that is happening." "Well, let's go see." In fact, I went to her house. This girl was still in bed: "Well, what's happened to you?" I ask her. She says: "I don't know." And her mother: "Look, look, the cut hair, the cut hair, a ripped camisole hanging on the chair . . ." I asked: "Tell me, was the door open or closed?" because I thought that maybe some youth had fallen for this girl and had come in during the night and cut her hair and ripped her camisole. But no, the door was closed, there was a latch, they assured me. I said: "Tell me something else, do you have some scissors on hand?" She said: "Why?" "Answer me." She says, "There is a scissor, but it's in the drawer," because I thought that this girl had cut her hair by herself. To prevent these nasty tricks the family had a *magaro* come, I think it was zio Rocco from Castello. He undid the spell, so that the girl recovered, and now she's married to a youth from Montemurro.

Cutting one's hair and ripping one's clothes are expressions of mourning: the girl from Castello evidently performed a theme of mourning or sorrow in a twilight state. Let us consider other data drawn from our field notebook:

Every day A. L., a peasant girl from Viggiano approaching her first menstruation, fell into a momentary crisis that lasted just enough time for her to make a cut on her dress in the form of a cross: immediately afterward, she "woke up," not realizing that she had done this gesture. Naturally the crises—which lasted for a certain number of days —were framed in the traditional interpretation of possession on the part of evil spirits, and the parish priest of Viggiano and, subsequently, a *fattucchiera* from Montesano intervened at the family's request in order to free the "possessed girl." This unconscious cutting of clothes is not an isolated case: in Pisticci we learned of many similar cases and likewise in other Lucanian villages. A girl about to be married cutting her own wedding dress is also widespread, in the same conditions of twilight state or total unawareness: here we need to ask if the impulse in this case does not express an aversion to the future husband and the imminent wedding, which will not seem strange if we keep in mind the traditional practice of "arranged" marriages in which the girl's satisfaction counts little. In general, episodes of sleepwalking are frequent. There is a common narrative of the woman who goes to the fountain at night to get water in a sleepwalking state, and the next morning does not realize that the bucket is full: in Roccanova, just such a girl had the nickname "the sleepwalker."

C. P., a sixty-eight-year-old peasant woman from Roccanova, related the following story: One evening in 1915, C. P. couldn't fall asleep. Her husband was away at war, and she was in dire straits, with two small children. While she was alone in her bed, restless and famished, she had the idea to get up and do some chores to get her mind off of her restlessness and hunger. She took a pitcher and went to the fountain to draw some water. It was in the middle of the night. Passing near the cemetery, she saw a figure dressed in white coming toward her, whom she recognized to be her dead mother. C. P. was not afraid; it seemed to her almost to be dreaming. The figure in white stood next to her and walked with her to the fountain in silence. On the way home she saw another figure in white. It was Vincenzo Cervino, a peasant who had recently passed away. Vincenzo told her to give his news to his wife, who was still alive and living in the village. Accompanied by the two figures, C. P. continued to walk toward her house, but at a certain crossroad the ghosts made off into the night. Once home, the moment she went back to bed, C. P. was "waking up," and it seemed to her "as if she had been in a dream." She looked around her: the pitcher full of water was there to prove that she had really been to the fountain. Experiences of this sort are relatively frequent among Lucanian peasants: "They're things that happen to us peasants," an informant woman from Roccanova once told us resignedly. What characterizes such experiences is the fact that they arise in moments of physical exhaustion or prostration owing to lack of food or serious emotional upset. The long treks at dawn to reach one's workplace play a preponderant role. A. V., a forty-year-old peasant woman from Roccanova, went to the fields in September 1953 with a group of six other coworkers in order to harvest figs. The group set out around midnight in order to be at the orchard by dawn. When the group arrived at a place on the road where some time previous a young peasant had died accidentally, it seemed to them that the figure of the dead man appeared in the shadows, then disappeared, dissolving into a column of fire. The group was overcome with panic and dispersed into the country-side screaming.

M. T., a seventy-year-old peasant from Roccanova, once saw a snake as she was crossing the road while walking to the fields at dawn. She killed it and hung it on a tree. That evening, on her way home after a day full of work in the fields she passed by the same place, where the snake was still hanging on the tree. As if she had had a premonition, she decided to bury the snake and she approached the tree to do so. But just when her held out her hands, the snake raised its head and said: "So you're not content with having killed me, you want to do me more harm by burying me?" From these words, M. T. understood that the snake was the soul of a dead person. Usually the character of such narratives is that of real psychological adventures: they are told as actually experienced personal events, with indications as to names, dates, and circumstances, and with the confirmation on the part of other people to whom the story was previously told.

A recurring hallucination in the Lucanian villages is that of the "Mass of the dead." A. T., an eighty-year-old peasant from Rotondella, was heading to the fields one night, and after some hours of walking passed in front of a monastery church: the door to the church was open and the inside was lit up. As soon as she entered, she immediately real-ized that she had happened upon a Mass of the dead and ran away. R. S., a sixty-year-old peasant from Colobraro, attended a Mass of the dead once when she was returning from the fields at night. Forty-five-year-old R. M., a peasant from Colobraro, witnessed a Mass of the dead one evening while she was drawing water from the fountain. One of the souls present, who was her St. John's *comare*,[2] warned her of the danger, saying: "Get out of here, it's not a place for you; if you don't go, you'll remain in it." R. M. ran away, but the hem of her skirt snagged on the leaves of the church doors and got torn. The same vision, with analogous conditions of onset (night, while drawing water at the fountain or while heading to the workplace) and with analogous dynamics (the St. John's *comare* who warns of the danger she is facing, and the detail of the skirt snagging on the door leaves) was told to us by several informants from Pisticci and Roccanova.

The temporary emergence of second personalities, with impersonations of corresponding characters, is a frequent episode, traditionally interpreted as a possession on the part of spirits or as a veritable demonic possession when the second personality is deviant, in conflict with the normal character of the subject and with any moral norm whatsoever. A. V., a fifty-year-old peasant from Pisticci, was the victim of twenty-two spirits from March 19 to May 23, 1956. According to her daughter's account, A. V. impersonated her various characters by taking on their voices, speech, and personality: they were generally people who had died a violent death.

Especially in a popular environment, the crisis of mourning in Lucania takes on extreme manifestations. In its most radical form, the crisis of presence presents the characteristic polarity of absence and convulsive release: the individual presence disappears, and the psychic energy is degraded in the pure and simple mechanical energy of the convulsions. The frequency of a reaction of this sort is incredibly high among the Lucanian peasant women and it presents various nuances and gradations according to the degree of absence and of the features of

---

2.   The reference is to the relationship of *comari di San Giovanni* between two women (*compari di San Giovanni* between two men). This was a ritually sanctioned form of close friendship that was widespread in many areas of Southern Italy and Sardinia and was related, along with godparenthood, to a broader system of fictive kinship. Unlike godparenthood, however, this institution has fallen into disuse in contemporary Basilicata. —Trans.

the motor release. In a much less radical form, the absence is attenuated in a state of stuporous dullness, or in place of the convulsions there is a terrifying, tendentially self-aggressive paroxystic explosion. The state of stuporous dullness among the Lucanian peasant women is so common that it is indicated with a term in common use in Lucanian villages: *attassamento*. The *attassata* person is rigidified in a physical immobility that reflects a real psychic block that is more or less pronounced. We find various nuances of *attassamento* outlined in the crude descriptions that several of our informants gave of it, and that correspond fundamentally to the reality of the psychic state as it appears to the observer. As an informant from Montemurro told us, "The *attassata* person doesn't recognize people: she doesn't remember that someone died. If you ask her something she doesn't answer, or else she give answers nonsensically. It's as if she were dreaming. When she comes out of the *attassamento*, she looks around to understand what has happened, then she cries out and begins her lament." An informant from Albano Lucano had this to say: "The *attassamento* can last a quarter of an hour. The *attassata* person doesn't answer questions or make any sense; when she comes to and realizes what's happening, she cries out and resumes her lament." Another informant from Albano said, "The *attassamento* comes above all when someone gets news of a sudden death. It can last half a day." An informant from Avigliano said, "As soon as she comes out of the *attassamento*, she gives a cry because she recognizes what has happened." The state of dullness is diametrically opposed to paroxystic explosion. If in her stuporous dullness the woman remains inert, without recollection of a mourning situation, in paroxystic explosion she throws herself on the ground, bangs her head on the wall, jumps, scratches her cheeks until they bleed, is lit up with a furor that tends to be directed toward herself; she pulls out her hair, tears her clothes, abandons herself to a cry in what is really more of a howl. In general these extreme manifestations of the crisis find a horizon and discipline in ritual lament.[3]

The fact that "evil eye" is also called "envy" is in obvious relation to the frequency of envious feelings in an environment characterized by the precariousness of the elementary goods of life. Moreover the belief that envy (and its curse) can be involuntary has a real basis in the

---

3.   On this, see de Martino (1958: 83ff.).

restrictedness and fragility of individual presence and in the fact that envious feelings can move in a sort of dusky halo without being able to bring them to the level of moral consciousness and control them. In this sense a real psychological situation of irrepressible envious drives corresponds to the secret evil that circulates in the air, to the "binding that goes on the road" (as the Lucanian spell says), from which at times not only the envied person feels the need to defend himself but also the envious person, reciting reassuring and exorcising formulas. Additionally, in conditions of particular fragility of presence, being envied by others becomes a disintegrating stimulus that also exercises negative psychological (or even psychosomatic) influences.

It is upon these conditions of presence's fragility that the *protective* function of magical practices grafts itself.[4] Lucanian magic is a complex of socialized and traditionalized techniques aimed at protecting the presence from the crisis of "psychological misery" and indirectly—that is, by virtue of its protection—reveal realistically-oriented operative powers. In an existential regime in which the power of the negative involves the center itself of cultural positivity—the presence as operative energy—the use of the technical power of man does not contain value and function in the profane sense of producing economic material goods, or the material and mental instruments to better control nature, but rather in the sense of defending that fundamental good that is the very condition of participation in cultural life, no matter how restricted. In the Lucanian existential regime, there is a particular importance not only in the negative—for example, as hunger or illness—but also in the much

---

4.   Here and in the paragraphs that follow, de Martino lays out his theory of magic's functioning through ritual de-historification. This theme is developed further in the next chapters of this volume, where the discussion is extended to religion. It is not possible here to mention all of the various exegeses of de Martino's theorizing of presence and ritual de-historification, but the reader may wish to refer to Marcello Massenzio's important treatment of de Martino's theoretical writings on the subject: see de Martino (1995b); Massenzio (1997). In English, Tobia Farnetti and Charles Stewart have translated a key essay by de Martino, accompanied by a translators' preface: de Martino ([1956] 2012). Fabrizio M. Ferrari's (2012) volume also discusses these issues. —Trans.

more serious risk of an individual presence losing itself, a presence that through its work must deal in a realistic sense with hunger or illness or any other critical situation of existence. It is precisely for this reason that even today in Lucania magical techniques are practiced that help the presence to reintegrate itself from its crises. The realistic level and the magical level of the technique do not enter into a subjective contradiction because magic does not really have as its object, as profane technique does, the suppression of this or that negative, but the protection of presence from the risks of existential crisis when faced with manifestations of the negative. As long as there is the need for protection, the conflict does not take place, or it remains purely ideal and oratorical: herein lies the reason for which the magical level basically remains "impervious to experience" and thus to both the failures of magical practices and the observation that the successes go hand in hand more frequently with realistic actions than magical ones.[5]

---

5. We must clearly reject the interpretation of magic's imperviousness to experience as an expression of a "primitive mentality": magic can be, as will subsequently be clarified, a more or less important moment in a society's religious life, but any human society belongs to history to the extent that it activates rational behaviors that are realistically oriented, and it opens to decisions and choices that have a profane and worldly sense. Moreover, magical behaviors do not at all document another logic, but only the adaptation of man's technical coherence to that particular end that is the protection of individual presence from the risk of losing itself. With regard to such functions, magical techniques bear a coherence that in itself is no less than that which is employed for the realistic control of nature and for producing material instruments. The ambiguity arises when we judge magic on the same level as modern science and with respect to the same objectives, with the result that we either are no longer able to distinguish magical practices and religious life itself from the deliria and aberrations of the human mind, or we postulate a "structure" of primitive mentality that "impedes" people from seeing how things actually are. Equally unacceptable are all those theories that aim to found magic on the reality of so-called "magical powers": without denying attitudes of this sort (although they are unusual and exceptional), we must keep in mind that they arise from the proximity of man to nature, and thus it would be better to speak of "impotencies" and not "powers." It follows that no human civilization has ever based itself exclusively on such attitudes, since civilization is the *ethos* of man rising up as a rationalizing presence in the heart of naturalness and

Magical protection, as emerges from the material regarding Lucanian magic, is carried out thanks to the institution of a metahistorical level that absolves two distinct protective functions. Above all, this level creates a stable and traditionalized representative horizon in which the risky variety of possible individual crises finds a moment of coming to a halt, configuration, unification, and cultural reintegration. At the same time, the metahistorical functions as a place of the "de-historification" of becoming: a place in which, through the repetition of identical operative models, the historical proliferation of happening can from one time to the next be reabsorbed, and thus amputated of its actual and possible negativity. As a stable horizon of the crisis, magic offers a mythical framework of magical forces, of bindings and possessions, of spells and exorcisms, and institutionalizes the figure of specialized magical practitioners; with this the various means of losing presence are embraced in configurations, symbols, in univocally defined systems of metahistorical influences, in prospects of first aid on the part of exorcists and healers. As a stereotypical operation of reabsorbing the negative in the metahistorical order, magic is more properly ritual, power of ceremonial words and gestures, permanent efficacy of a certain tangible material (for example, the *abitini*). With this, the historical variety of the resistances and the negative aspects of becoming get traced back to the repetition of a same resolving order, in which the negative is "naturally" always suspended or annihilated. Indeed, on the metahistorical level of magic, all pregnancies arrive splendidly to term, all the newborns are alive and well, milk always flows abundantly from the mothers' breasts, all illnesses are healed, all of the uncertain prospects are defined, all storms go unleash themselves in the desert, and so on—precisely the opposite of what actually happens in history. By virtue of the metahistorical level as a *horizon of the crisis* and place for the *de-historification of what is coming to be*, a protected regime of existence is instituted that on the one hand shelters from chaotic

---

establishing himself as an autonomous person, present to himself and to the world, while those attitudes either follow suddenly from the unconscious or are provoked by partially submerging oneself in it (as in trance and similar states). Thus we are not denying that a magical practice can, for example, facilitate a hunting party's good results, but no civilization could ever give up on actually hunting: the hunters of the Paleolithic never simply opted for magical drawings of animals with arrows piercing their bodies.

eruptions of the unconscious, and on the other veils what is happening and allows one to "be in history as if he weren't in it." By virtue of this double complementary protective function, individual presence is maintained in the world and goes through real critical moments or faces the real uncertain prospects "as if" everything were already decided on the metahistorical plane according to the models that it exhibits. Yet even within this protected regime of existence, the fundamental good to protect is reintegrated: the individual presence, which in fact goes through a critical moment or faces an uncertain prospect, opens itself to realistic behavior and profane values that the crisis without magical protection would have compromised under such conditions.

CHAPTER NINE

The horizon of the crisis

With regard to the horizon of the crisis, the fundamental framework of Lucanian magic is made up of themes of magical powers, binding, possession, spells, and exorcism. The metahistorical level acting as a horizon is thus depicted as an evil power of persons or mythical entities defeated by another power of other people or mythical entities. The experience of *being-acted-upon* is the risk of crisis for which this horizon offers arrest and configuration. Being in the world—maintaining oneself as an individual presence in society and history—means *acting* [*agire*] as a power of decision and choice according to values; it means always performing anew the never-definitive detachment from the immediacy of mere natural vitality and rising to cultural life. The loss of this power and even the spiritual possibility of exercising it, represents a radical risk for a presence unsuccessfully engaged in resisting an attack in the form of the experience of *being-acted-upon*, where *being-acted* involves the personality as a whole and the operative powers grounding and supporting it. To illustrate the pathological experience of *being-acted-upon*, let us examine the "feeling of emptiness," the delusion of influence and states of possession. Feelings of emptiness, so thoroughly analyzed by Janet, consist in the loss of authenticity of self and the world, where the flow of psychic life is accompanied by a sensation of alienation, artificiality, unreality, and distance. This sensation strikes one's thoughts, feelings, and actions as well as the experience of objective reality (persons, events, things, situations).[1] Although these experiences of emptiness and depersonalization can be variously interpreted by the sufferers—and in fact they are more or less limited in duration and more or less elective with regard to certain psychic contents—there is a single basis underlying them: the actual loss of presence. Consequently, from a productive condition regarding single problems connected to acting according to single forms of cultural coherence, *being in the world* itself gets transformed into an empty problem; it gets transformed into a pure asking without a real will to reply, into an ineffectual and anguishing existential doubt that wraps itself up in the misery and inactivity of its sheer asking and doubting. In its physiological condition, the ego decides within certain operative values, and the productive problems of thought and action always concern its self-realization in action that bears an objective quality and cultural meaning. In the pathological condition of depersonalization and the emptiness, the risk instead appears to be that of not being able to emerge from the situation as a power of decision and choice, and thus the very "ego" itself becomes a problem in an immediate way, as does the "world." This is an empty and irresolvable problem that repeats and underlines the process of moral disintegration, whereby the presence gets emptied of effective resolving means.

The experiences of emptiness and depersonalization analyzed by Janet include the possibility of a development in the direction of a "domination" and an "influence." When the presence enters into crisis due to the collapse of the sheer possibility of making itself the center of decisions and choices according to values, one may on the one hand have the experience of an "empty" self and world that are inauthentic for various reasons. On the other hand, though, the sufferer's ineffectual compulsion may be oriented toward a depiction of whatever is doing the emptying and dispossession: a sui generis occult and evil alterity rises to face the presence in crisis. The latter is qualitatively different from an ordinary alterity featured as a negative dialectic moment in the unfolding of cultural coherence's operative powers. This *radically other* element taking the shape of an evil agent to be corralled within the operative circuit of presence—and that in the meantime maintains itself in a riskily eccentric

---

1. Janet (1926–28). A typographical error lists the author as "J. Janet."—Trans.

mode with respect to any possible human behavior—is the other face of finding oneself "emptied of self," "other from the self," and inauthentic, in an alien and artificial world. Or, to put it differently, as an experience of the personality's disintegration, *being-acted-upon* features one possible attempt at defense in the definition of an occult agent operating on a level that is different from the historical one. Some of the narratives reported by Janet attest to as the passage from a state of emptiness and depersonalization to the experience of an influence and a persecution that proceed from a supernatural and metahistorical force. In the first narrative, depersonalization is reflected in the experience of a spatial dislocation of personhood: "I am not in me: I feel like I am behind my shoulders, to the left, at greater or lesser distance according to how sick I am" (Janet 1926–28, vol. II: 79). In the second narrative, the self dislocated in space as if it were other appears to be in the process of becoming an other that commands: "I hear myself speaking, and it is someone else speaking, I am surprised to reply the way I reply. . . . I am no longer in control of what I do and think, I am being led" (Janet 1926–28, vol. II: 53). The third narrative clearly demonstrates the passage from a state of emptiness to the experience of an alterity that is already beyond the normal or historical order, saying, "Everything in me is a dead letter, I am no longer a woman with a heart, I've been loaned the soul of another, I am nothing but a poor marionette whose strings are being pulled everywhere, my soul is being stolen, I am constantly changing owner, behind the wall there is someone I belong to, and who disposes of my thoughts and actions" (Janet 1926–28, vol. I: c). Someone "beyond the wall" who "steals the soul": here, we are already touching upon the theme of the evil and occult force that "enchants," "binds," "ties," or "attaches." As for "stealing the soul," this very expression frequently returns in the world of the so-called primitive civilizations to designate precisely the riskiest effects of enchantment, so that one of the witch doctor's tasks is to capture stolen souls and return them to their proper owners.

But the most fertile ground for the development of a delusion of influence and persecution is to be found in mental illnesses, which, like paranoia of influence and schizophrenia, construct their delirious imaginings in an interpretative function of *being-acted-upon*. In the paranoia of influence, the psychosis begins as a psychic hallucination or more rarely a psycho-sensorial one, with thoughts and feelings that are perceived as not being one's own or immediately participating in the personal current of psychic life. For example, one of Georges Dumas' patients had the feeling "of a physical and mental domination of his own person: he was obliged to stop, he was directed, he was impeded from moving his arms or from doing this or that" (Dumas 1947: 216ff). In the beginning, all sufferers are irritated and astonished by the symptoms they experience: then, with the onset of pseudo-hallucinations, with the proliferation of automatic movements, and with painful and strange sensations growing more and more acute, "a whole part of their being appears under the domination of someone else" (Ibid.: 112). In schizophrenia we find the same experience of the self's disconnected alteration and alienation. One of Henry Claude's patients declared: "My thoughts run their course in spite of me: my spirit is empty, my brain is not normal, the fluid that is in me makes me abnormal, it is changing me and modifying me bodily" (Janet 1926–28, vol. I: c). A schizophrenic of the Saint Anne Psychiatric Center in Paris documents how a delusion of influence can be grounded in a real loss of self and the alienation of presence: in order to signify the invisible "forces" operating on him, this patient had coined certain neologisms, with which he sought to adapt language to the extraordinary experiences of his own psychic disintegration. Combining *attraction* and *hantise* [obsession], he invented the neologism *attises*, with which he designated the compulsive or hidden stimuli that burdened his thought and action. Among the various manifestations of these *attises*, the patient attributed particular importance to the *vents électiques*, that is, to the mysterious blowing and pushing that caused him to feel like he was no longer the master of his own thoughts and feelings, and even of his very soul. These *vents électiques*, which were among other things responsible for some mysterious voices, operated irresistibly though a special device, the *pousse-dieu*, so named because it "pushed the soul to God" (Dumas 1947: 218).

Finally, we must consider states of possession. When the presence's margin of autonomy is restricted to such a degree that it disappears, and when a second aberrant and perverse personality suddenly appears on the scene, substituting itself for the historical consciousness for a more or less prolonged period, one has a state of pure possession. The crisis intervenes in a spontaneous and improvised way, and the return of historical consciousness is followed by total amnesia. By then, the victim of the attack no longer has the experience of *being-acted-upon*, because the presence rests without margins for appreciating the attack itself. There is an actual interruption in the duration of personal consciousness, a gap in which a personality acts in stark contrast to the normal one and all of the rules of moral life and behavior in force in a given society, so that the *being-acted-upon* is manifested only from the point of view of those who witness the crisis, but not that of the victim. Nonetheless, the state of possession presents various shades and nuances in which the presence under attack does not remain entirely without margins, but witnesses, writhing in vain in sterile attempts at recovery and faced with a devastating eruption: in this case, one has a lucid possession that stands in relation to pure possession as a siege that one does not manage to break stands to the wholesale occupation of the besieged place.[2]

These psychopathological data help us to understand the nature of the risk for which the metahistorical horizon of Lucanian magic works as an instrument of arrest, representation, and unification of the variety of possible individual crises of presence in the face of an unleashing of the negative's power. The ideology of magical power, binding, possession, enchantment, and exorcism offers a representative framework that is stable, socialized, and traditionalized, in which the risk of alienation of single presences is converted into a metahistorical order, a level on which the recovery and reintegration of risk can be carried out. Moreover, the recovery and reintegration of risk can take place to the extent that a current or possible negativity of becoming can be ritually de-historified. In this way, a second protective moment of magic takes shape: the myth as an effectual *exemplum* of happening and ritual as repetition of the myth.

---

2. Cf. Oesterreich (1922). The distinction between *possessio* and *obsessio* dates back to mystical theology: cf. Paulain (1906: 423).

Chapter Ten

De-historifying the negative

In Lucanian magic, the de-historification of becoming—or more pre-cisely, of what is happening as current or possible negativity—takes place through the basic technique of "just-as" [*così-come*]: the "just" of a certain concrete negative feature and of a corresponding desire to eliminate it gets ritually absorbed within a resolving mythical exemplification. This exemplification takes on various degrees of complexity and representa-tional autonomy in relation to the ritual performance, but no matter how rough and rudimentary it is, it is never lacking. When women at the river fill a placenta and recite the spell "just as this bag gets filled with water, so may these breasts be filled with milk" [47], they mime and recite an elementary myth in which filling the placenta with water reabsorbs a host of critical individual moments related to nursing. When erysipelas is enjoined to leave and it is announced that silver is arriving, whose contact it must flee [23], one mimes and recites the exemplary myth of silver that makes erysipelas flee, so that when the silver is ritually placed in contact with the illness, the erysipelas escapes into the high sea [24, 25]. Ordering a *rànula* (sublingual cyst) to run away receives its magical sense from the mythical *as* with which the spell opens: "on a little moun-tain peak there were four oxen that crushed the head of a frog" [42]. In other Lucanian spells, the metahistorical model repeated in ritual dis-plays with words and gestures features a negativity that goes away just as it came, whose beginning and end are laid out, as are its doing and undoing. With this, the historical negativity—whose origin, course, and outcome are uncertain—gets de-historified. The myth of the headache is the sun that sets, leaving the headache, and rising again takes it back [12, 13]; the myth of jaundice is the rainbow that gives jaundice and reabsorbs it [33], and the masonry arch on earth reiterates the arch in heaven ("blessed holy arch, you're written in heaven and earth") [34] and substitutes the rainbow in the ritual; the myth of erysipelas is a metahistorical erysipelas that enters and exits from one Friday to another [26]; and the myth of intestinal worms is the Holy Week, in which the metahistorical rhythm, with its beginning and end, reabsorbs the single concrete historical situations related to this disorder [39]. In all these cases, the narrating and miming ritual repeats exemplary myths in which everything has already been decided in the desired direction. The mythical moment becomes even more explicit and autonomous in the so-called *historiola* spells, whose negative beginning and end are reshaped into exemplary episodes that have metahistorical practitioners as protagonists of the "doing" and the "undoing." In the spell for breast engorgement [51, 52, 53, 54], the metahistorical exemplification tells of a deformed dwarf that in *illo tempore* does and undoes the engorgement, provoking it in the women to avenge their mockery, and then undoing the spell after they apologize. The ritual is thus the stereotyped repetition of this univocal *exemplum*, whose exemplary stability absorbs the various uncertain concrete possibilities of single cases of engorgement as they arise. In spells 16, 17, 18 and 19, the doing and undoing are entrusted to two distinct mythical agents, one evil and the other benevolent: the harmful agent is the evil wind, while the good one is nameless and faceless in the versions from Ferrandina, Pisticci, and Savoia, whereas in the one from Oppido the exorcism is carried out in the name of Jesus, the Madonna, and the saints. This spell is connected to a pagan formula discovered in Carnuntum (present-day Petronnel in Southern Austria) in a sealed sarcophagus from the third century CE. Written on a rolled silver leaf that made up the sarcophagus' accouterments, the spell reads as follows: "For migraine headache. Antaura rose from the sea complaining like a deer, mooing like an ox. Artemis Efesia came to her: 'Antaura, where are you going . . . ?'" In illustrating this fragment of a spell, Barb (1926) underlines how Antaura should be interpreted in the sense of a "malignant wind": this leads us back to the "evil wind" of the Lucanian texts. As for the benevolent agent, Artemis Efesia appears substituted by Jesus, as the Greek papyrus of Paris 2316 demonstrates, and in fact Jesus appears in the Oppido spell together with the Madonna and the saints, while in the versions from Ferrandina, Pisticci, and Savoia the wear of time has rendered the figure of the mythical exorcist anonymous, or has even—in the cases of Pisticci and Savoia—reduced the formula to a simple exorcistic command without an explicit and autonomous narrative pattern.[1] The spell against the evil wind is related to the group of Christianized spells, whose corresponding *historiolae* feature saints or even members of the Holy Family as agents. Likewise, in the spell for stomach ache [27–32] the metahistorical model follows the scheme of the deformed dwarf who carries out his evildoing in response to an offense, and he undoes it after amends have been made. In the spell for stomach ache, however, the offence is that of inhospitality to a saint or sometimes even to Jesus wandering in disguise, so that the saint (or Jesus) punishes the inhospitable woman with stomach ache, only to free her of it thanks to her husband's intercession [29, 30, 31, 32]. Other spells connect a variety of critical situations to the metahistorical sameness of exemplary healings performed by saints or sometimes Jesus himself [27, 28]. Even the myth of Christ's death and resurrection is subject to this reduction on an elementary level of magical exemplariness: the raising of Christ on the cross thus gets reduced to the model of a headache's getting up (or going away) [14]; the mythical significance of the Redeemer's blood, spilled

---

1.   Cf. Barb (1926: 54f.) and Reitzenstein (1926: 176ff.). The spell is featured in Pradel's collection, *Griechische und süditalienische Gebete, Beschwörungen und Rezepte des Mittelalters*, "Religionsgeschichtliche Versuche und Vorarbeiten" (15ff.). On the "encounter" spell belonging to the oldest mystical literature, see Peterson (1926: 109ff.). With regard to the fact that the spell appears to be used in contemporary Lucania for urticaria and not for migraines, we must keep in mind that both migraine and urticaria can have a neurotic basis (cf. Finichel [1951]: 285ff. and 288ff., Italian translation): this can probably help us to understand the transposition of the spell's use and even, in certain conditions, its psychosomatic efficacy in both cases.

to wash away sin, is linked to the restricted function of an *exemplum* in order to wash away jaundice from the sufferer's blood [35].[2]

When the negativity is not present but is something possible that concerns the future, the technique of *just-as* takes the form of prefiguring models, the inspection of signs, forbidden behaviors, and reparatory rituals. For an accurate understanding of this technical form, which is quite widespread in Lucanian magic, it is necessary to keep in mind the psychological meaning of a possible negativity in a regime of existence in which crises of psychological misery are particularly prominent. Here, the risk of losing presence takes the shape of the risk that the prospect of the negative installs itself in consciousness and becomes parasitic, where all of the other contents of consciousness become allusive or symbolic with regard to the feared event. In particular, all behaviors take on a significance that prefigures that event, following analogies that are not at all coincidental. In relation to this, forbidden behaviors multiply and action gets punctuated by meticulous interdictions that, carried to an extreme, lead to an actual paralysis of action. Magical ideology protects from this risk thanks to the institution of culturally accredited metahistorical horizons in which a prefiguring meaning is recognized only for a certain few behaviors. By virtue of this choice of mythic symbols, only some behaviors get forbidden, while others remain available for profane needs. Additionally, the metahistorical horizon is not limited to choosing the prefiguring symbols and to establishing forbidden behaviors, but also embraces the ritual that undoes or in any case repairs the forbidden behavior that was carried out inadvertently or because of

---

2.   On the spell that exhibits the blood of Christ as an *exemplum* for regenerating human blood, cf. Pradel (1907: 135 [in Latin]; 24 [in Sicilian dialect]). On spells with a *historiola* and their ecumenical diffusion, cf. van der Leeuw (1933, and more briefly 1956: 482ff.). Cf. Mircea Eliade (1949), *Le mythe de l'éternel retour*, especially pp. 63ff. It is necessary to be aware, however, that in every magical practice, and not only in spells with *historiola*, there is always a metahistorical *exemplum*, even though this does not imply the articulation in definite mythical figures, nor the autonomy of an actual narration of some resolving episode. Even a spell with an extremely poor mythical horizon, such as the one that recites the last letters of the alphabet [41], displays the *exemplum* of a series that ends with and with this exemplary ending reabsorbs and cancels out the negative.

necessity. This gives rise to a protected regime of existence in which the negative prospect is cancelled out by virtue of a mythical *as if* whose model gets rigorously reiterated both in the interdictions it involves and in the reparations it commands. Burning the wood of a wild pear tree is a mythical symbol for rough and prickly skin; passing under a rope and crossing hands around a chair back are mythical symbols of an umbilical cord twisted around a neck; passing near a carpenter who is sawing wood and stepping on wood shavings is a mythical symbol of *sertedda*; a butchered pig that has lost all its blood, a fish associated with the absence of blood, and dried cod are all mythical symbols of a malnourished child (p. 30); and so forth. It is sufficient that the myth be respected in the positive and negative behaviors it requires (for example, not passing below a rope and passing back in the opposite direction if the action has inadvertently been performed), and the unlucky prospect is reabsorbed into a metahistorical horizon where there are no adversities, or where the negative is always cancelled out due to the simple reason that it has already been nullified. Finally, in divinatory practices the theme of the de-historification of possible negativity is attenuated, where the inspection of prefiguring symbols is aimed not so much at nullifying the undesired possibility as much as it is at suppressing the uncertainty of the future and prefiguring it. The negative, in this case, is the very uncertainty of the prospects. In this technical framework we find the inspection of signs during baptism (pp. 33–35) or during the wedding ceremony (pp. 11–12), as well as the divinatory ceremony for the various possibilities regarding the fate and the faithfulness of a loved one far away [11].

CHAPTER ELEVEN

Lucanian magic and magic in general

If we limit ourselves to considering "Lucanian" magic in its moments of the risk of *being-acted-upon*, the metahistorical horizon of a force that binds and possesses, and the de-historification of the negative through the ritual repetition of an identical resolved myth, we realize that such a protective system has nothing in and of itself that is historiographically identifiable. In one measure or another, with a greater or lesser degree of diffusion, with different elaborations and cultural mixtures, a magic of the "Lucanian" type is still present today in numerous folkloric areas of modern civilization, variously influenced by hegemonic cultural forms.[1]

---

1. For example, magic still has significant survivals in the contemporary German Federal Republic. In West Berlin, a "Deutsche Gesellschaft Schutz vor Aberglauben" [German Society for the Protection from Superstition] was recently founded, while in Hamburg we have the publication of an "Archiv zur Bekämpfung des modernen Hexenwahn" [Archive of the Campaign Against Modern Belief in Witches]. Cf. Schmidt (1956); Krause (1951). From a legal and criminological perspective, see Schäfer and Wendte (1955); from a medical perspective see *Der Landartz* (1955/13) and (1956/36), *Deutscher Medizinischer Informationsdienst* (1955/7), *Die Medizinische* (1956/39) and (1957/2) and (1957/5). Police reports are equally noteworthy: cf. *Deutsche Polizei* 1954/12. In 1957 the social importance of this question led Lower Saxony's ministry of social affairs to charge the sixty-nine public health councils to carry out an investigation

We find a "Lucanian" type of magic among so-called primitive peoples, although among the latter it is more widespread and complex, and it features a higher degree of integration with the rest of cultural life. Keeping in mind this reservation, we can easily adapt to "Lucanian" magic many ethnological reports regarding magic in civilizations studied by ethnologists. For example, we have Strehlow's report regarding magic among the Aranda of Central Australia:

> The sorcerer's art consists in particular in neutralizing the influence of hostile men or evil beings. He is called in serious cases, whether the illness has been caused by hostile people or instead by a demonic entity. . . . The natives attribute all illnesses to external influences, to men assisted by black magic who claim to be able to cause the death of another person, or to demons who in the form of animals or natural phenomena (for example, in evil winds) approach a man and cause him harm.[2]

---

of witchcraft in the region. Besides rural witchcraft, a form of "cultured" magic continues to enjoy a certain credit in today's Germany, featuring a most ambiguous mix of scientism, exoticism, irrationalism, and superstition: this has given rise to cultural phenomena that potentially constitute an instructive document for the history of customs. Consider the advertising bulletin of the "Laboratorio chimico farmaceutico Giulio Chrometzka" in Fleestadt near Hamburg, a company founded in 1875 that is fully active today: this laboratory offers its clients, among other things, "magic-occult novelties, sympathetic medicines, magical powders for fumigations, preparations from all corners of the globe for occult studies and for transcendental experiments," and this to aid people who intend to practice white magic but also to assist the concentration of intellectuals, writers, et cetera. Among the products displayed is a Mexican tincture of Peyotl, good for clairvoyance and telepathy; the Indian Yogi perfume that induces states of trance and is useful for experiments in hypnotism and clairvoyance; an "astralograph" to get into contact with the great beyond, an apparatus constructed after thirty years of experiments; single amulets in precious metals and stones, with fine engravings according to one's horoscope or date of birth (from 95 to 150 Marks), and so forth.

2.   Strehlow (1907–20: 28, 40); cf. Spencer and Gillen (1927: 397). For a survey of binding among primitive peoples, see Webster (1948: 151). Cf. *Mondo Magico*, pp. 129ff.

Just as we saw for Lucania, we find themes of magical force and binding, death spells, and exorcism, and even an "evil wind" as an obscure
demonic entity. Features of "Lucanian" magic, moreover, are present in
a wide variety of historical epochs and civilizations. Lucanian binding
recalls Greek *baskania* and Roman *fascinum*,[3] and even Christian demonology admitted binding as an effect of a tacit or explicit pact with the
devil, as proved in particular by the theorizations of Innocent VIII's famous bull *Summis desiderantes affectibus*, of the *Malleus Maleficarum*, and
in general of the vast demonological literature connected to the bloody
persecutions against witches during the sixteenth and seventeenth centuries.[4] As for states of possession and the corresponding exorcisms and
"therapeutic" rituals, these forms all have a place not only in the magic of
primitive peoples (especially in shamanism),[5] but also in all religious civilizations, whether they are currently existing or have disappeared. Keeping to a perspective of time and culture closer to our own civilization's,
the Greek terms *mania, oistros, lyssa, oribasia, entheos* are all clearly linked
to experiences of this sort,[6] and in Christianity itself possession and

---

3. Kuhnert, in *Realencyclop.* Pauly-Wissova, VI, pp. 2089ff. [This citation was
    incomplete in the original text. —Trans.] See Pauly et al. (1894).

4. In particular, on the literature relative to binding from the dawn of Chris-
    tian civilization to the sixteenth century, see the work of Lynn Thorndike
    (1929–1941); especially vol. II: 553, 574 (Alberto Magno), 607 (Thomas
    d'Aquino), 901 (Pietro d'Abano); vol. III: 432ff. (Nicola Oresme); vol. V:
    475 (Antonio Cartaginese), 486 (Francesco Perez Cascales); vol. VI: 528
    (Leonardo Vairo). See also the treatment of binding and various types of
    evil spells in Martino del Rio, *Disq. Mag. Lib.* III, Quaest. IV, Sectio I-X, a
    work that achieved a certain notoriety, as evidenced among other things by
    the credence given to it by Manzoni's Don Ferrante.

5. On possession among primitive peoples—besides Oesterreich (1922: pas-
    sim)—see Webster (1948:180ff., 195, 210f., 361ff.). On possession in sha-
    manism, see Eliade (1951: 333ff., 399ff).

6. Recently H. Jenmarie (1951: 105ff. and 157ff.) has given proper promi-
    nence to the theme of mania and maenadism at the heart of Dionysian
    religiosity, on the one hand demonstrating the connection of such psy-
    chic states to contemporary forms (Sudanese and North African *bori*,
    Abyssinian and Egyptian *zar*), and on the other hand making an explicit
    comparison between possession phenomena and the so-called "great attack"
    of the Salpêtrière school. For a survey of the forms of possession in various

exorcism were included in the Gospels, and the exorcist became—as is
well known—one of the four minor orders.[7] We must also keep in mind

---

magical-religious civilizations, the aforementioned work by Oesterreich,
Die Besessenheit, remains fundamental. With regard to the Ancient Greek
world, particular attention has been paid to the relationship between possession and Corybantism: see Ivan M. Linforth (1946a: 121–62).

7. On the passage of the ancient world's ideology of possession to the Christian one, cf. for a comparison of the documentary data, Tambornino (1909).
For a modern Catholic point of view on the question, one should consult
Lhermitte (1956) (It. trans. 1957; Lhermitte is full professor at the Faculty
of Medicine in Paris), de Tonquedec (1938) (de Tonquedec is the official
exorcist of the diocese of Paris), as well as some articles contained in the
volume devoted to Satan, *Études Carmélitaines* (1948). In general, from a
Catholic point of view the problem of diabolic possession arises first and
foremost in mystical theology as a theory of the devil's possible action "on
the point of intersection and union of body and soul," and thus in psychiatry
as a collaboration and division of tasks between the psychiatrist and the exorcist. Secondarily, it arises with the choice of criteria for distinguishing false
possessed, who are simply ill, from "true" ones held to be really tormented by
the devil; finally, it is present in the exorcist's actual practice. A reflection of
such a conception in missionary practice is the interpretation of possession
phenomena in missionary lands as a manifestation of the devil's resistance
to the spreading of the faith (cf. P. Laurent Kilger, O.S.B., in *Études Carmélitaines*, cit.), while a more proper historical-religious reflection of this
conception is the attribution of a belief in the devil, strictly speaking, to the
most ancient hunter-gatherer and nomadic pastoralist civilizations, since a
belief in the devil "presupposes one in a supreme being," and only in these
civilizations is such a belief strong. In primitive agricultural civilizations and
in secondary and tertiary civilizations, instead, we speak of "spirits" or even
"evil spirits," but not really of the devil as the adversary of a good God, the
Supreme Being (P. Jos. Henninger, s.v.d., *L'adversaire du dieu bon chez les
primitives*, in *Études Carmélitaines*, cit.). It is necessary to note that from a
historicist point of view, all of this categorizing is senseless due to the simple
reason that it excludes a priori, for religious reasons, the possibility that the
"devil" is a human cultural product to be treated entirely within the drama
of single religious civilizations. Moreover, what one should think of the "one
God" of Catholic theology antihistorically transferred to primitive peoples
following the well-known thesis of the Viennese branch of the historical-
cultural school (where for now, to complete the picture, the devil of Catholic
theology should undergo an analogous transposition), has been—it seems to
us—clearly demonstrated in Pettazzoni's work on God's omniscience. On

the ecumenical spread of the technique of de-historifying the negative through the ritual reabsorption of negativity on the metahistorical level of a resolving myth, of an implicit or explicit *historiola*.

The folkloric data regarding Lucanian magic thus lead us to structurally analogous phenomena that are manifested on an widespread scale in very different historical environments, even if with varying degrees of importance and integration in their respective cultural environments. This analogy and persistence in and of themselves form a problem that requires a solution. The monotonous repetition of the ideology of magical forces, binding, possession, exorcism of mythical models of de-historification, and the corresponding de-historifying power of the rite as such: all this seems rather scandalous for historically-oriented thought. Indeed, with its ahistorical replication, this ideology—simultaneously "Lucanian" and generically folkloric, primitive, and ancient, medieval Christian and of the period of the witch trials—seems to challenge any historicist orientation whatsoever that aims at identifying unrepeatable processes of human history, dramas lived out only once in cultural life.

The reason for this apparent ahistorical character is to be sought above all in the fact that magical force, binding and possession, spells and exorcism all have their roots in a risk that underlies cultural life, and which concerns the very possibility of being here as a presence in human history. In this sense, the repetitions and uniformities of magical elements need to be traced to the constant of the existential risk of *being-acted-upon*. This is a risk that the moral force of culture dominates and resolves with an agency that is open to value. Magic repeats itself in human history and seems to act more like a natural fact than a human act because it is rooted in a risk that involves the naturalization of psychic life in its extreme form as a fall in presence's transcending energy. But the apparent ahistorical quality of magic could also depend on a methodological error: that is, when we isolate magical protective techniques from the concrete cultural context in which they carry out a protective function and we compare them to other, similar techniques present in other cultural contexts, in order to end up by showing a type

---

the period of the witch trials, besides the famous work Soldan and Heppe (1911), one should also see the essay by Brouette (1948) and the bibliography on pp. 658ff.

of "magical world" that in such a fictitious isolation has never existed **as a cultural fact.** The historical sense of magic's protective techniques lies in the values that such techniques reveal, grafting themselves onto the critical moments of a certain regime of existence, and it is therefore manifested only if we consider these techniques as a **moment** of a perceptible cultural dynamic within a *single* civilization, a *particular* society, a *certain* period. Once we commit the methodological error of artificially isolating the magical moment from a certain cultural context in motion, and once we head down the path of abstract comparison of magic's protective techniques wherever they appear as techniques, we lose the criterion for distinguishing magic as a moment in cultural life from magic as a technical impulse that fails (consider, for example, those magical features that appear in schizophrenia, the paranoia of influence, and compulsive neurosis). Actually, feelings of emptiness, delusion of influence, states of possession, and compulsive rituals cannot be confused with magic as a cultural moment for the simple reason that the defense techniques they develop do not reveal any order, mediate any real integration, or effectively open up the presence to reality and its values; instead they amount to a sterile, private impulse lacking a horizon. A progressively delusional detachment from reality is evident in the case of the schizophrenic who attributed the cause of his feeling of being dominated within to the *attises* and *vents électiques*. But we also find a detachment from reality when the agent is individuated in existing historical forces such as the Company of Jesus or Freemasonry, since it is evident that such forces are bent in the delirium to a merely private use, without a real correspondence to their real historical function and without any tie to the cultural consciousness we have of them. To the contrary, in the regular functioning of magic as a moment of a certain cultural life in a specific society, we do not have ineffectual, individual impulses, but socialized and traditionalized technical systems through which the experience of *being-acted-upon* gets subtracted from the ineffectual judgment of empty individual imagination, mediating its reintegration into cultural reality and its values. Certainly the change whereby *being-acted-upon* opens itself to *agency* may not take place in magic: so the "case" does not directly interest the scholar of cultural phenomena and the historian of religious life (it might be of interest only to the extent that it underlines the moment of risk), and returns to falling within the competence of the psychiatrist. Psychiatrist Georges Dumas recalls that in 1913 a family from Neuilly formed a typical delusional threesome, in which the husband believed he was under his mother's spell, and his wife shared this conviction, as did his mother-in-law. The threesome had a consultation with a *fattucchiera*, who gave them some wise advice, though she had them carry it out in a rather eccentric manner: she suggested to the three to raise a photograph of the famous psychiatrist Gilberto Ballet to the summit of a pole, and to head outside the reception desk of his clinic shouting at the top of their lungs, "*Redoute Gilbert Ballet! Il est très fort contre les diables*" ["Renowned Gilbert Ballet! He is very strong against devils"]! The doctor on call, who was brought in immediately, in fact sent them to Ballet, who subsequently utilized the threesome as clinical cases to illustrate his lessons to students. Adding to the confusion was the fact that the three, who had already been hosted by other psychiatric clinics, had picked up on the scientific terminology used by the doctors to try to define their case: the husband thus said, in reference to his own psychic condition, "my automatism," and the wife and mother-in-law confirmed, "his automatism," or "his mental disintegration" (Dumas 1947: 286). A case like this makes it clear that even when terms of spell and enchantment appear in a delusion of influence, and even if there is a traditional consultation with a *fattucchiera*, the delusion of influence remains as such and does not get confused with the normal functioning of magical techniques in a specific society. The confusion does not take place because what is missing is what actually gives a cultural sense to these techniques: their mediating a progressive reintegration into reality and its values. We have proof that magic as a moment in a certain cultural dynamic is not isolatable as a separate group of techniques in the fact that every time someone has attempted to write a history of single magic techniques or even of magic in general, it has never gone beyond a vast compilation of cases indiscriminately drawn from primitive populations, from the ancient world, from religions of the Far and Near East, from the Middle Ages or the period of the witch trials, and finally from contemporary folklore[8]: this is a collection dominated by the monotonous

---

8.   The attempt of the Viennese branch of the historical-cultural school to retrace the origins of magic in an obscuring of primitive monotheism does not deserve to be mentioned if not as an example of cryptogamy between

repetition of aberrant cases, in which quite often one does not understand how exactly they differ from corresponding clinical cases illustrated by modern psychopathology. For example, the old work by F. T.
Elsworthy (1895) on the evil eye[9] is based on the assumption that this
belief's origins are lost "in the obscurity of prehistory" and it should
therefore be considered "as an original and hereditary persuasion of humankind" (Elsworthy 1895: 3); that is, precisely as something "ahistorical" par excellence, belonging more to the biological order of human
nature than to the cultural order of history. In a subsequent work by
Seligmann (1910) on the same subject,[10] despite the fact that its subtitle
announces it to be a "contribution to the history of superstition of all
times and of all peoples," it is in fact only a compilation that collects data
and classifies it, at times according to race, at times according to the
quality of the binding entities (single individuals, social groups, animals,
monsters, supernatural entities, inanimate objects), and at other times
according to diagnostic criteria and therapeutic means, and so on, with
further subsections and subdivisions of the subsections, ranging among
ecumenes and jumping from one millennium to another. We could make
similar reflections about "historical" works on possession, for example
the aforementioned work by Oesterreich, whose survey encompasses
primitive peoples, antiquity, the Middle Ages, and modern times, with
frequent references to psychopathological data from the French school
(Azam, Janet, etc.). In Oesterreich's work, too, the analysis is merely clas-
sificatory, and the material is grouped according to "symptoms" of
possession, the psychic state of the possessed, the ways of ending the
possession through exorcistic practices, the geographic and ethnic

---

the apparent impartiality of positive research and confessional needs, which
are inherently very partial.

9. In the original text de Martino wrote the name mistakenly as "Elworthy."
    —Trans.
10. Seligmann was an ophthalmologist who, in his positivistic prejudice, be-
    lieved himself to be particularly qualified to deal with "evil eye": and even
    more recently, another ophthalmologist, Edward Gifford, believed by virtue
    of the same prejudice that he should deal with the same topic (cf. Gifford
    1958). A strictly typological essay is that of Tuchmann (1884–85) "La fas-
    cination," in *Mélusine* II (cf. E. Mancini [1887]: 675ff. [the original text
    reads "Mangini" —Trans.]).

distribution of the phenomenon in its "spontaneous" as well as its "induced" and "controlled" forms.[11] The historiographic indifference of magical techniques in general was naively recognized by Hutton Webster in his work on the magic of primitives. Excusing himself with his readers for having chosen a relatively limited documentary basis for establishing magic's elements as a human cultural fact, he allows himself this declaration, which for us is quite instructive:

> To trace [magic's] history and enormous influence in the civilizations of the modern age would be a task calling for the cooperation of a galaxy of scholars. My humbler task has been to set forth the chief principles of magic, and these are as well exemplified in rude communities as in those of higher type. Indeed, there is little or nothing in the magic of old Egypt, Babylonia, India, and China, of the Christian West, and the

---

11. Cf. Oesterreich (1922). We cast the same judgment upon the work of de Félice (1947), which is nonetheless permeated by a noble civil inspiration, since the author's polemic against "gregarious" or "crowd" states appears to be conducted against gregarious states connected to totalitarian regimes, specifically Nazi rallies, with their refined techniques aimed at weakening the sense of moral responsibility of single individuals. Moreover precisely this suggestion has induced the author to consider "lower" forms of mysticism more generally under an almost exclusively gregarious heading, one that is also basically pathological, with the result that everything is placed on the same level, from possessed primitives to the patients at the Salpêtrière, from the energumen and possessed of the Christian period to the participants of Nazi rallies, without the narration ever taking on a proper historiographic profile. The author insists in his work on the fact that human personality has an essentially "precarious" character (de Félice 1947: 364), and that "although it exists virtually in each of us, it is nonetheless a continuous acquisition, a conquest that we must defend ceaselessly, since from one moment to the next it can be taken away from us" (364; cf. 177); and he rightly observes that personality remains firm to the extent that it opens to "moral and spiritual" forces (87). Precisely for this reason, however, an essay on the lower forms of mysticism (as the author calls them), and in particular on the gregarious states or madness, can only lead to a sort of gallery of horrors or—in another sense—to a list of clinical cases. Thus the disintegrating techniques of Nazi rallies are doubtless a part of European cultural history, but only if we connect them to the movement of that history, according to a specific historiographic problem.

Moslem East, which cannot be duplicated in savage Australia, Africa, and America. Magic is as thoroughly primitive as it is cosmopolitan. (Webster 1948: ix)

Now, if the historiographic indifference to magical techniques is pushed so far that we can take the results obtained on the basis of documentary material from primitives and generalize them to all civilizations and all periods, this simply means that the magical techniques are not historicizable, and that no "galaxy" of scholars will ever succeed in transforming into a cultural process what has by virtue of comparative abstraction been systematically amputated of various historiographically accessible meanings. The magical moment takes on meanings and manifests them only according to historical civilizations, periods, and environments, so it is only within the religious or moral history of these civilizations, periods, or environments that the magical moment receives its rightful place in cultural dynamism. As further proof of the correctness of this thesis we should keep in mind that the most mature historiography has always made an effort to qualify the magical moment within a specific civilization or epoch, and in function of some cultural value that constitutes the real center of historiographic research. In this regard we might recall what magic represented in the Renaissance according to the interpretations of Burckhardt, Cassirer, or de Ruggiero, or the insightful observations of Garin, who frames Renaissance magic, both ritual and "natural," as a break in the closed medieval universe, and who takes it as a mediator of the infinite possibilities of nature and the infinite demiurgic power of man.[12] One might also recall the essay on Bacon by Paolo Rossi, which presents an analysis of the highly exemplary moment of the passage from magic to science, one of the fundamental themes of the foundation of modern civilization (Rossi 1957).

---

12. See Garin (1954: 150ff.; magic and astrology in the Renaissance) and (1954: 170ff.; reflections on magic).

CHAPTER TWELVE

Lucanian magic and Southern Italian Catholicism

The reflections of the previous chapter help us to move beyond the wholly artificial isolation of the data regarding "Lucanian magic." This isolation is solely the result of our ethnographic abstraction, for which we ourselves have isolated the data from their cultural context. It is obvious that every abstraction of this type only has a temporary character and at a certain point requires a reintegration into concrete life and its dynamics if we want to pass from describing to understanding. If we reintegrate "Lucanian magic" into the Southern Italian society of which it is a part, and into that modern world in which Southern society is in turn inserted, the corresponding data gradually lose the isolation in which the abstraction held them. A whole series of relations and connections become visible, along with intermediate moments that serve as a bridge to hegemonic forms of culture, and which reestablish the communication from low to high that was interrupted by the hasty cutting of the abstracting procedure. In this way, in place of "static" surviving data, we obtain a cultural "dynamic" in which the magical practices illustrated in the ethnographic section constitute certainly the lowest, crudest, and most elementary moment, but are not such a lost island in the ocean at an immeasurable distance from the continent as we might be led to imagine. Precisely these relationships, connections, intermediate moments, and communication from low to high rescue "Lucanian magic" from the empirical reality of its geographic contingency and from a mere curiosity for the picturesque, as well as from the irrelevance of meaning for which the corresponding data simply appear as practices of superstitious little women and as detritus destined to disappear in a very short span of time in the face of the vigorous assault of modern civilization.

Actually the "survivals" of Lucanian magic or generically Southern magics do in fact "live" in some fashion and absolve, in their societies, a function of their own. As long as they "live"—even if only for circumscribed human groups—they maintain some coordination with the hegemonic forms of cultural life, starting with the hegemonic religious form of Catholicism, with its often emphasized Southern accents of "exteriority," "paganism," and "magic." This helps us to recognize that "Lucanian magic" is not limited to a few restricted relics as would seem to appear to those who, more or less imprisoned in a confessional polemic, consider the spell for breast engorgement to be pure magic and the recitation of the rosary to be pure religion.

If we consider the spell for breast engorgement, in which a deformed dwarf performs and undoes the curse, we are doubtless dealing with one of the most restricted forms of Lucanian magic. The restriction regards first and foremost the magical technicality that gives a horizon only to a very particular mode of existential crisis and de-historifies a single, very particular aspect of the negative, exhibiting an *exemplum* whose use is valid only for that aspect. Second, the restriction concerns the mediated value, which does not go beyond the moral sense of trust and endurance that arises from experiencing the illness "as if" one had already been healed. If we now consider the spell for migraine, in which a mythical exorcist—once Artemis Ephesia and in Christianity, Jesus himself—operates against the devil, or if we take the spell against stomach pains, in which a saint or Jesus first punishes and then frees the inhospitable woman, we barely perceive the passage to a slightly "higher" level of magic. The de-historifying power of the formula remains restricted (it deals only with those very particular aspects of the negative manifested as migraine and stomach pains), but in the meantime a mythical Christian horizon appears along with the figure of Jesus as the exemplary exorcist. This opens at least a possibility for somehow participating in a

mythical horizon whose de-historifying of possible aspects of the negative goes much further than the model of Jesus as exorcist, and whose efficacy in mediating values infinitely exceeds the endurance of a migraine
or stomach pains. We can make analogous considerations for the spell in
which Christ raised on the cross serves as a paradigm for the getting up
or going away of the headache that weighs on the eyes, or for the other
spell that exhibits the Redeemer's blood as resolving *exemplum* for blood
sick with jaundice. Even here the great mythical theme at the heart of
Christianity loses luster within the straits of *historiolae* that are only valid
for circumscribed aspects of the negative; nonetheless, the very fact that
the theme appears in these *historiolae* constitutes at least the possibility of
confusedly recalling the values that it mediates. The clergy, whose direct
or indirect influence is responsible for these manifestations of syncretism
and readaptation, intuited the pedagogical function of the connection
that came to be established in certain conditions, if only on an elementary level. The clergy therefore allowed the pagan spells to be opened or
accented by signs of the cross or prayer, in imitation of Christian exorcisms, and it substituted Christian *historiolae* for the pagan ones. It even
attempted to substitute actual mnemonic expedients for the *historiolae* in
order to fix Christian religious themes in people's minds, as in the case
of the spell against storms recorded in Viggiano [55]. Other connections
between magic and the hegemonic form of religious life are blatant in
folk Catholicism, in private extraliturgical prayers, in the cult of relics, in
the course of pilgrimages to the Marian sanctuaries of Viggiano, Pierno,
Picciano, and Fonni, in miraculous cures, and in everything else in the
Lucanian area that reflects a particular meaning of "exteriority," "paganism," or "magic" of Southern Italian Catholicism. Yet we must not forget
that this "magic" is at least potentially a mediator of Christian values,
even if only in an extremely limited and elementary way, and even if the
mythical images evoking these values can in fact be restricted in consciousness to a series of *exempla* that are basically similar to the *historiolae*
of the spell for breast engorgement or jaundice.

Through the connections and nuances discussed above, Lucanian
magic communicates with the fundamental themes of the Catholic cult,
with the sacramental and the sacraments—in short, with the sacrifice of
Mass itself. It does so through a continuity of moments that, again potentially, mark a gradual approach to the heart of the Catholic religion,

where the specific folk or even "Southern" nuances of Catholicism get partially dissolved and in part attenuated and sublimated, to the point of reaching what characterizes Catholicism as a particular Christian confession. Nonetheless the "magic," no matter how attenuated and rendered a mediator of high values (at least for those who are capable of experiencing them), never completely disappears, since—if we consider it from a general theoretical point of view, and outside of any confessional polemic—no matter how "high" religions are, if they are truly religions and not merely moral life, knowledge, or poetry deployed and rendered autonomous in conscience, they always contain a mythic-ritual nucleus, a public "exteriority" or "showiness," a magical technique in action, even if it is refined and sublimated. Thus from the extracanonical exorcism of *stregoni e fattucchiere*, we pass to the exorcisms of the missal (blessing water, salt, prayers against Satan and other evil spirits at the end of the Mass, etc.), of the pontifical (dedication of churches, the blessing of holy oils and bells, etc.), and of Roman ritual (the ritual of baptism, blessing of wine, oil, gold, incense, and myrrh, medals of Saint Benedict and especially the *de exorcizandis obsessis a daemonio*). Although canonical exorcisms are sacraments instituted by the church on the model of exorcistic operations carried out by Jesus and the apostles, and although their efficacy is produced *ex opere operantis Ecclesiae* and therefore without the character of infallibility that the sacraments have, we should note that their practical reduction to the level of extracanonical exorcisms is in fact always possible for those who ignore Catholic theological distinctions and, de jure, there is a magical nucleus in canonical exorcism even in the very way that Catholic theology theorizes it. Indeed, canonical exorcism takes as its model the figure of Jesus as exorcist and works to drive out the Devil regardless of the intentions of the priest and the subject, by virtue of the power that Jesus has bestowed upon his Church.[1] Precisely because it has an exorcist-Jesus as its model, canonical exorcism undoubtedly reveals all of the values in which this God-Man is a symbol. It is also true that the theory of canonical exorcism underlines the

---

1.   On canonical exorcism, besides the works cited in the previous chapter (n. 4), see Bartmann (1956, vol. I: 402ff., vol. II:150, vol. III: 68ff.); Maussbach (1957: 218); Tanquerey (1928: 1545–48, 1957: 709ff.); Vagheggini (1957: 330ff.).

need to not test God with a belief in the effect's automatism, and in the case of freed energumens, it foresees prayers of thanks to the Lord and the commitment to avoiding sin so as not to fall back under the Devil's sway. Precisely this margin left explicitly to moral personality hints at the loftiness and complexity of the mediated values, but it does not in any way entail superseding the mythic-ritual technical structure of magic. In particular, the connections of the magical moment with the exorcistic values of baptism are demonstrated by those extracanonical exorcisms in which "baptized" flesh is exhibited, like the *historiola* which, on a mythical level, reabsorbs the influences of the evil force of binding [1, 2, 3].

This continuity of degrees and passages from the crudest forms of Lucanian magic to higher and more complex forms of hegemonic religious life finally extends to the sacrifice of the Mass. The corresponding section of the Council of Trent and the treatises of dogmatic theology tell us that the sacrifice of the Mass is the representation (or re-presentation) of the sacrifice of the Cross. Having "historically" taken place only once, this sacrifice is rendered concretely present in every Mass, and in each Mass it becomes contemporary to the original event. Effects of adoration and thanks to God proceed from the Mass *ex opera operato*, and effects of expiation, propitiation, and supplication *per modum impetrationis*. If we compare the Mass's structure to that of the spells with *historiola*, we again find a fundamental magical nucleus of the mythical horizon of the crisis and the de-historification of the negative on the exemplary level of the myth, and at the same time an opening to value. There is undoubtedly an immense cultural distance dividing the extracanonical exorcism of "Lucanian magic" from the sacrifice of the Mass: but this distance only concerns the degree of complexity of the magical technique and the quality and degree of autonomy of the mediated values. The extracanonical spell of Lucanian magic is a mythical horizon that refers to a specific existential crisis, and it is an instrument for de-historifying a circumscribed aspect of the negative. As noted above, the value it mediates does not go much further beyond a generic moral security generated by dealing with that circumscribed mode of the negative *as if* it had already been reabsorbed in the resolving myth. The sacrifice of the Mass instead gives a horizon to an indefinite number of technical operations of de-historification that can be carried out on this horizon: the sacrifice of the Mass is to extracanonical spells as—and the comparison does not seem out of line—an electronic calculator is to a child's abacus. From the point of view of values, within the liturgical drama itself we find the possibility, each time, of experiencing the exemplary efficacy of the sacrifice of the man-God who came one time to remove sin from the world. In the shadow of this precise eruption of the divine into history and under the protection of a sui generis passion that has reabsorbed all worldly suffering and has brightened itself with themes of resurrection and the second, definitive *parousia*, the Mass nourishes Christian virtues of faith, hope, and love flowing beyond the confines of the liturgical event, and shaping Christian custom in the multiple, profane relations that are a part of the world of men. If we thus look within the series of connections and passages that from the lowest level of ceremonial magic rise to the heart of the hegemonic religious life, that being the Mass, we always find a mythic-ritual technical moment that gives a horizon to the crisis and carries out the de-historification of the negative, opening up the sphere of "value" to one extent or another. Thus, only in relation to the straits of technique and above all the poverty of values do we speak of "magic" with regard to the lower level, just as only in relation to the complexity of the mythic-ritual moment, and above all to the loftiness of the values mediated, do we speak of religion with regard to the Catholic cult. This, however, is equivalent to recognizing that the moment of religious opening and mediation of values, however tenuous it may be, is never absent, even in the crudest *historiola* spell. In just the same way a magical nucleus is never missing from the celebration of the Mass itself, at least inasmuch as the sacrifice of the cross is an *exemplum* that becomes present in a sacramental way and to the extent to which the Eucharist—as an objective means of grace—works *ex opera operato*. As proof of this evaluation *ab intra* of the dialectic magic-religion nexus, we may note that even the sacrifice of the cross can be situated within very narrow horizons for those who attend Mass with intentions that are not far from those in which an extracanonical exorcism normally gets recited. Indeed, the raising of Jesus on the cross and the Redeemer's shed blood can transform themselves in *exempla* for headache or jaundice. Moreover, even the spell for breast engorgement, which features the *exemplum* of the dwarf that performs and undoes the curse, can in certain cases rise to some degree in the religious sphere if the person reciting it does not limit herself to gaining a renewed sense of confidence in life, but instead through ritual repetition allows it to mediate some elementary sentiment of inner sympathy and reverent submission for the deformed dwarf who, derided by the group of women, nonetheless forgives them and frees them from his vindictive curse, once he has received an apology.[2]

---

2. Every other attempt to ascertain the relationship between magic and religion on the basis of an interpretation of the experience of the sacred that breaks the real dialectic connection of this relationship and exalts a pure religion without a trace of magic or condemns a pure magic without a trace of religion, is the stuff of confessional polemic. Religious historiography always narrates a dynamic that from existential crisis passes by way of the mythic-ritual technical moment to open up to the world of values. The traditional antithesis between magic as a ritual "constraint" conducted by the magician, and religion as "submission" to a higher reality and a moral relationship with divinity, is in itself schematic and superficial, since even in the lowest ranks of magic ritual words and gestures draw their efficacy from the repetition of an exemplary myth, and it is the *exemplum* recited that is actually efficacious and not the mere automatism of gesture and word, which as such would get confused with a pathological automatism. On the other hand, the highest form of religious life, rich with complex moral values, can deteriorate in rough souls—or in moments of inner misery that even lofty souls sometimes experience—into restricted, scrupulous ritual performances. Second, even in the crudest forms of magic there is a relationship with higher forces, spirits, and entities that are more or less mythically formed, and the domination of these forces on the part of the magician is never absolute and automatic, because his activity depends on higher helping spirits, and because there is always the possibility of obstacles on the part of more powerful hostile forces. To the same extent as religion, elementary as it may be, magic always entails both a reintegration into values, otherwise it would be existential crisis and illness. The only legitimate meaning of the distinction between magic and religion concerns the loftiness of the mediated values, the degree of awareness and autonomy of these values, and their penetration in the mythic-ritual technique whereby we can say, comparatively speaking, that religion is an experience of the sacred in which the mediated values are high and complex, with a high level of awareness and autonomy and permeating myth and liturgy. The "submission to the divine" of religious life has a double moral meaning: the recognition of a reality of values that transcend individual selfishness and to which man—if he does not want to live like a beast—must submit himself, and the recognition of the negative that can indeed be reabsorbed on the metahistorical level of myth-ritual, but not in the absence of a morally-oriented human behavior. And nonetheless, if we do not want to abuse

This methodological framework for the relationship between "Lucanian magic" and Southern Catholicism entails a quite severe critical evaluation of the Protestant conception of a pagan South, the preferred land from which to draw fodder for an anti-Catholic polemic. With regard to Southern Italy's religious life, Protestant writers have generally spoken of an ongoing paganism and a Catholic church that is, *sic et sempliciter*, pagan as well. The most important work reflecting this hermeneutic criterion is that of Theodor Trede on paganism in the Roman church (1889–91), carried out with material drawn almost exclusively from the religious life and customs of the regions that formed the Kingdom of Naples. The author's thesis is that the church did not defeat Greco-Roman paganism, but quite to the contrary, paganism defeated the church: "old wine has remained in the skin, only the label has changed" (Trede 1889–91, vol. I: 313ff.). Trede is forced to admit that folk "superstition" is not so specific to the South, since it exists everywhere; but he immediately adds with his usual emphasis that in the land where "golden oranges shine among obscure foliage," it takes on the proportions of a giant, while in Germany it has those of a dwarf

---

the term "religion," any religious life—no matter how lofty it is—remains anchored to a mythic-ritual technical nucleus, even if it is refined and sublimated. To the accusations of Protestants and "rationalists" regarding the magical character of sacraments, Catholic theologians usually rebut that the sacrament is not a holy spell, detached from the recipient as well as Christ, and operating through its own power. We must observe, though, that strictly speaking absolute spells do not exist in any magical practice, no matter how low it is, precisely because the efficacy of any spell does not depend on the magical practitioner alone, but also—and especially—on the more or less explicit *exemplum* recited in the ritual and on the lack of intervention of more powerful forces. Moreover, the efficacy of the *exemplum* recited is perceptible even in the sacraments and in the sacrifice of the Mass. Undoubtedly Protestants and "rationalists" too often forget that the "interiority" of the relationship with the divine, carried to its logical conclusion, leads not to religion but to the dismissal of mythic-ritual technique and to the recognition of the autonomy of profane values; they too often neglect to recognize the lofty values that Catholic sacrament can mediate in elevated souls, to whom it is not enough to simply "not place obstacles" or "not close the door" to Grace's entrance. Even so, this does not change the fact that Catholic theologians are wrong when they reject the magical moment of their religion's sacraments.

(Trede 1889–91, vol. I: c, vol. IV: 373).[3] The proof of such an openly polemical and confessional thesis is based on the exhibition of magical, superstitious, and pagan data from the folkways and religious life of Southern peoples and on corresponding erudite commentaries that, case by case, refer to antecedents in the ancient world. The work opens with the description of the temple of Poseidon in Paestum, highlighted by this emphatic statement: "The temple of Paestum lies before us as a dead remnant of Paganism; the pages that follow intend to locate its living remains in human life" (Trede 1889–91, vol. I: 2). Indeed, a sort of living museum of the horrors of Southern religious life unfolds before the reader's eyes, with long, erudite digressions aimed precisely at demonstrating that nothing has changed since the time of false and deceitful gods. The author's attitude is unvaryingly one of making a show of covering his face and raising a cry of horror as he gradually reveals to himself and to others the monstrous spectacle of an unprecedented *Kulturschande*. The first revelation is undoubtedly rather disconcerting:

One's pen hesitates when it is obliged to write things that the author knows will not appear credible to the reader. And the fact that I am about to refer is certainly incredible: the Eternal Father is known only among a limited segment of the Southern population; he is paid honor only by a negligible number of people in the city of Naples, and there is only one place in the Southern regions where one encounters his cult—that is, in only one of the hundreds of churches in that city. (Trede 1889–91, vol. I: 23)

After the peremptory observation that "God almighty is far from the Southern Catholics" (Trede 1889–91, vol. I: 31), the author passes to ascertain what is instead close or very close to them, and the reply is unvarying: Greco-Roman paganism. The chapter on the Sanctuary of Montevergine and the prodigious image of Mamma Schiavona[4] yields

---

3.   Compare, as an ironic comment to this haughtiness, note 1, pp. 109–110, concerning present-day Germany.

4.   "Mamma Schiavona" is the name given to the black Madonna of Montevergine in local popular tradition. The image corresponds to that of the Madonna della Candelora, whose sanctuary is located in Mercogliano in

the usual reduction of the Marian cult to pagan mother goddess (vol. II: 85ff.); the festival known as the *Madonna delle galline* in Pagani[5] offers the occasion for an erudite comment on Demeter and Ceres and the ritual sacrifices that accompanied the cult (vol. III: 206ff.); Saint Anne is compared to the Greek Hera and to Roman Juno, since for the women all three stand for "the same thing" (vol. II: 148). The magic of holy water, incense smoke, flowers on the altar, lights placed before images, vows, relics of every sort; images and statues in such an abundance that in Naples it is easier to meet a god than a man: all this is pagan (vol. I: 15). The guardian angels are genies (vol. II: 66ff.), the *monacello* is connected to the lares and the penates (vol. II: 196ff.),[6] and so on, until we reach the most blatant legacy from the ancient world: the cult of snakes that is still alive throughout the South and especially in Calabria (vol. II: 48ff.); the witches, possessed people, exorcist priests, and extracanonical exorcists known in Sicily as *caporali* (vol. IV: 353ff.); evil eye and *jettatura* and so forth (vol. II: 226ff.). It is clear that a work of this sort would not even deserve the honor of critique if it did not eminently represent a type of evaluation of Southern Catholicism that, in the absence of historical-religious works on the subject, significantly influences common judgment—the polar opposite of the other type of evaluation, that of a pious and devout South and of an extremely religious Naples. We should immediately note that every reduction of magical-religious life in the South to the ancient world's paganism is bound to remain a simple argument for confessional polemic or a superficial touristic impression: the most elementary historical sense alerts us to the fact that ancient

---

Campania. Folklore scholar Ferdinando Mirizzi generously provided this information in personal communication. —Trans.

5. The festival of the Madonna del Carmelo, known popularly as the "Madonna delle Galline [Madonna of the Hens]" takes place annually in the town of Pagani in the province of Salerno. It features many elements common to Southern religious festivals, but the event is distinguished by the presence of various sorts of birds—hens, roosters, peacocks, doves—that participate in the rituals and accompany the statue of the Madonna as it is carried in procession. —Trans.

6. The *monacello* is a gnome-like trickster spirit in Southern Italian folklore, often thought to be the spirit of a child who died unbaptized; the lares and penates were ancestral household deities in Ancient Rome. —Trans.

paganism, with its complex mythic-ritual world, with its articulations and differentiations in diverse and distinct religious civilizations that were variously mediating of values, is completely dead everywhere, and it would be useless to believe that we have rediscovered it in the South and in Southern Catholicism with its particular characteristics and nuances. For someone who proposes to reconstruct particular aspects of religious life in the ancient world, the indications of corresponding folkloric remnants would undoubtedly take on a certain documentary value—in specific cases and when particular caution is employed: that is what I myself have attempted to do with reference to ancient ritual lament (cf. de Martino 1958). But for those who aim to comprehend the religious life of modern Southern society, the question of "detritus" is not paramount, because what is central in this case is the analysis of how and why there is a certain web of communications and interconnections in Southern society from *lower* to *higher* levels, from the subordinated and fragmentary toward the hegemonic and unifying. This analysis should never lose sight of a dynamic that refers to the modern world, even if it involves moments of arrest, contradiction, detours, and lapses. We would search in vain for the features of Magna Graecia in contemporary Southern society, for the simple reason that to one extent or another Southern society has participated in the movement of Christian civilization and modern civilization. Our task is instead that of determining the actual extent of this participation and to glean from it a resulting picture in which the data regarding "Lucanian magic" and "Southern Catholicism" find a place.[7]

---

7.   It is not my intention here to examine each of the various Protestant writers who have dealt with the religious life of the South, and there is even less space in the present work for an analysis of the varied foreign literature, Protestant and not, which from the second half of the eighteenth century includes references to this topic. These travel books, for which it would be good to have a systematic treatment in relation to the foreign judgments of Southern Italian Catholicism, are in general useful for determining the way in which an Enlightenment or romantic European sensibility reacted in contact with the religious world of the South. Such a reaction indirectly helps us to measure in this sphere certain forms of "backwardness" of Southern society, which are spoken of too much in generic terms or under the immediate influence of partisan passions. Here, I limit myself to noting

Though concise, the analysis of the connections of Lucanian magic with the particular magical accents of Southern Catholicism and the magical nucleus inherent in the Catholic cult as a whole already hints at a perspective that is much broader than the strictly regional or local one from which we have begun. This perspective widens further and begins to take on its exact historiographic meaning when we pass from the importance of the magical moment of the South to another series of connections and intermediate formations in the heart of Southern Italian secular high culture, and we proceed to measure the participation of Southern thought in the choice between magic and rationality, wizardry and science, and exorcism and experiment, which constitutes one of the fundamental themes from which modern civilization was born. It is precisely here in the sphere of such participation that we find— with respect to the corresponding movement of European thought— certain delays in development, limits to the expanding force, and gaps and compromises that are highly instructive for a general evaluation of

---

that, in contrast to the work of Trede, Mayer (1840) touches on the subject of Neapolitan religious life several times, abandoning himself to the freshness of impressions and lacking the erudite pretensions of Trede. We read with interest his observations on the emotional and poetic element of folk devotions, on preachers like Padre Rocco, on the feasts of Sant'Antonio, San Gennaro, the Madonna dell'Arco, Corpus Domini, on spirits and witches, and so forth. Disagreeing with P. J. Rehfues, who in his *Gemälde von Neapel und seine Umgebung* (1808) emphasized the superstitious and magical aspects, Mayer instead insists on the tenuousness of the belief in witches and spirits that belongs to the "cloudy North," and he even states that "the lucid intelligence and happy character of the Southerner repels (witches and spirits) despite all of his ignorance." This judgment, which is the opposite of Trede's, demonstrates the limits of every impressionistic framework of the problem of the magical-religious life of the South, and the uncertainty and inconclusiveness that arise as soon as the traveler attempts formulate generalizing evaluations from particular impressions. Apart from exaggerations, things blown out of proportion and brash, erudite digressions, the work with the richest suggestions on the subject remains Alexandre Dumas' *Corricolo*, upon which I shall return below. [In the original text, de Martino mistakenly cites the author as "C. A. Meyer"; while the Italianization of Christian names was a common practice among scholars in de Martino's day, the surname is misspelled. Here and elsewhere, the name has been corrected to (Karl August) Mayer. —Trans.]

a cultural dynamic in which crude "Lucanian magic" and the magical accents of Southern Catholicism represent the most clearly negative aspect. Generally, in every modern society whatever remains lowest in the scale of cultural values, the wreckage of the past and the burden of delayed mental formations, and in particular the prominence held by magical techniques, all call into judgment precisely what lies highest among hegemonic forms of culture. They invite us to verify pretensions to hegemony and truth and to coherence and expanding, unifying force. In the same way—as Croce recalled at the end of his *History of the Kingdom of Naples*—to the "good men of Naples" who implored King Charles of Anjou for mercy for the city's revolt, and who excused themselves by saying it was the work of madmen, the King asked severely, "And what did the wise men do?" Indeed, in this widened perspective, a singular contrast appears at first glance: precisely in this angle of Europe, geographically designated as Southern Italy and politically as the Kingdom of Naples up to 1860, with thinkers like Bruno and Campanella, themes of thought flashed on the scene that played a significant role in breaking the tradition of medieval ritual magic and demonology, and through "natural magic" they opened the way to the sense of the man's demiurgic possibilities. Precisely in this corner of Europe, in Naples, from the second half of the seventeenth century to the end of the eighteenth century—precociously with respect to other regions of the period—the Enlightenment movement developed and produced works of European-wide importance. Precisely in this corner of Europe, Vico's reflections on the primitive and the barbaric mediated a sense of historical reason that, as a precursor to the historicism that unfolded in the subsequent century, initiated a human rethinking of man's varied cultural agency; this rethinking elevated itself from feeling without perception to feeling with a troubled and strained spirit, and finally to reflecting with a pure mind. This is, nonetheless, one of the areas of Europe in which the most intense contrast appeared between the peaks of high culture and the abundant evidence of archaic popular mental formations that not only formed a "magic detritus" in a strict sense but also influenced and colored Catholicism itself in a particular way. This contrast—which to the political man and educator poses specific practical problems for a more active participation of the Southern Italians in the broader movement of modern civilization—stimulates the historian to carry out and explore a series of specific studies within the framework of a **religious history of the South**.[8] This is a religious history conceived as the exact measurement of the participation of Southern thought in the great opposition between magic and rationality, so important—as mentioned above—for the birth of modern civilization. I intend here to bring a modest but not irrelevant contribution to such a rich history of problems, illustrating a specific process: the transformation of traditional binding into a product of ideology and folkways that began in Naples around the end of the 1700s and spread from Naples to the rest of Italy under the name of *jettatura*. The analysis of a minor process in the heart of the late-Neapolitan Enlightenment appears particularly instructive for the purpose of measuring certain limits of the participation of Southern culture in the conscious choice made by modern civilization to favor rationality against magic.

---

8. The Southern Italian ethnographies forming de Martino's great trilogy (*Morte e pianto rituale, Sud e magia*, and *La terra del rimorso*) must be viewed within this unifying framework of a religious history of the South. De Martino's early training as a historian of religion later melded with his ethnological interests, and he brought Benedetto Croce's idealist historicism together with a critical historicist perspective influenced by Gramsci. By locating himself within this framework, although he was dealing with cultural forms commonly considered folklore, he distinguished his approach from those of the dominant schools of folkloristics in his period. —Trans.

CHAPTER THIRTEEN

Magic and the Neapolitan Enlightenment
The phenomenon of jettatura

In the magical-religious civilization of the so-called primitive or ancient world—just as in the folkloric remnants of the crudest ceremonial
magic—unintentional binding and deliberate spells, the sorcerer's curse,
traps laid by spirits and demons, possession and exorcism, amulets and
counter-spells, inspection of signs, and divinatory practices all form part
of the same ideological order, whose importance and function within the
more general framework of the religious life of a specific civilization or
period needs to be assessed for each case. If, however, we want to find a
first cultural awareness in human history that binding has nothing to do
with magical forces strictly speaking, but with facts that belong to the
natural and profane sphere, we need to turn to Greek thought. Here, we
find—within the Sensistic tradition and Democritus' materialism—the
first outlines of a physical theory of binding as linked to effluvium or
emanations that detach themselves from the bodies of the binders. Here,
too, are the first beginnings of a psychological theory that represents
binding as the product of "images" that are launched from the eye and
the gaze with a charge of envy or evil, whereby the action of these material particles or "images" provokes misfortunate alterations in the victim's

body and soul.[1] We find magical-demonological interpretations and physical and psychological theories of binding throughout the Middle Ages, in various combinations and with different nuances: but in keeping with the development of Christian demonology and the attribution of magical wonders to the Devil, binding in this period maintained a predominantly diabolic or bewitching cast. This situation underwent a radical change in the epoch of the great crisis of ceremonial magic and demonology in the Renaissance and in the Reformation. As Garin has insightfully observed, in the Middle Ages low magic and more cultured versions lay at the margins of a thought that still held the cosmos in an immutable order governed by God. In the Renaissance, the choice between rationality and obscure forces, which seemed in the Middle Ages to have been definitively resolved, returned to the fore of consciousness with all of its extant energy, and it hinted at the quest for a new order and a new arrangement. Natural magic broke through medieval rigidity and raised man to being an explorer and demiurge of a malleable cosmos, chock full of secrets and occult powers; in this way the alternative was opened up between exorcism and experiment, between ritual and science. In the Middle Ages the church managed with some difficulty to keep the agitation for a greater religious interiority within its folds; during the Reformation, it was precisely on the point of the interiority of the divine, which in another sense and another direction constituted an antimagic and antiritualistic position, that a clamorous rupture broke the unity of the Christian world. In the Middle Ages the low magic of witches and cunning folk continued to survive among the masses without the ideological and repressive forces of the hegemonic culture issuing out a battle cry against it. In the Renaissance and Reformation, low ceremonial magic was hunted, dragged into tribunals, judged, and condemned both in the Catholic and Protestant worlds; moreover, in the judges' fanatical belief, judgment and condemnation got confused with the reality of tacit and explicit pacts with the devil. Certainly, a memorable battle against ceremonial magic and witchcraft was fought even

---

1. Plutarch. *Symposiacs.* V, 7M; Heliodorus. *Aethiopica.* III, 7 (cf. IV, 5 and Alexander of Aphrodisias, *Proble, phys.* 2, 53). [This citation was incomplete in the original text. See Heliodorus (1967) and Alexander of Aphridisias (1990). —Trans.] See Thorndike (1929–41, vol. I: 217).

through this secondary route, a battle that mobilized all of the repressive forces of ecclesiastic and secular courts.

Even the ideology of binding participated broadly in this vast, dramatic process that united themes of such a different development and that were apparently independent or even contradictory. Binding returned on the scene of cultural choice and once again created an open problem. On the one hand, in the confessional and repressive sphere, the demonological interpretation took on particular importance. Consider the example of Leonardo Vairo from Benevento, a canon regular of the Order of St. Benedict, doctor in holy theology, Bishop of Pozzuoli from 1587. In his volume *De Fascino* (1589), he considers binding "a pernicious quality induced through demonic arts, by virtue of a tacit or explicit pact with demons." Del Rio lists binding among the curses that entail the devil's intervention. With this, a theological tradition that had never been interrupted was reaffirmed, but with a vigor and an effort that can only be explained by recalling that this was the height of the period of the merciless persecutions of witches initiated nearly a century earlier with the papal bull *Summis Desiderantes* and with the *Malleus Maleficarum*. Conversely, in the sphere of "natural magic," the predominant interpretations were oriented in a natural sense that left demons out, and they appealed in various ways to celestial influences, to the spoiling of air by the binder's visual rays and spirits, or to the power of imagination and emotion. None of these motivations were new, but in Renaissance natural magic they took on a new meaning, especially with regard to the power of human imagination and passion. Indeed, all told we find here one of the expressions of the renewed awareness that the human spirit has virtues that can modify the physical world, which in turn is not inert material, but of an animate, sensitive, and excitable nature, and thus ready to have its forms produced or dissolved by a strong passion and by the lively imagination that inflame the heart and mind of man, as reflected in his eye and gaze. However, such an approach entailed a continuous passage from a psychological interpretation to a cosmological one and the uncritical acceptance of ancient beliefs connected to ceremonial magic and demonology, as can be seen in the following passage from Campanella:

> The eye manifests many magical things, because when one man meets another, pupil to pupil, the more powerful light of one man disorients

and strikes the other, who cannot withstand this, and often the former transmits the passion that he has on his patient: lovers transmit love, angry people transmit their scorn, upset people transmit their sadness; but it does not last long and the passion is not stirred. They say that the basilisk kills with its gaze, because it exudes ardent and poisonous spirits that we drink in through our breath and our eyes; it is held that it smothers with its power, because if it looks at a small tree or a child with affection, it causes its death. One who looks at something with admiration arches his brows and wishes to open his eyes as wide as possible to take in the admired thing, in order to know it and enjoy it better. Through this widening of his eyes, he sends out spirits that are very greedy for the desired and admired thing, and these spirits are immediately transferred with tenderness [toward the desired or admired person or thing] through the [skin's] pores, and they immediately act [in the recipients] with the same force with which they acted inside of the person who generated those spirits. [...] In this way, the spirits of the small tree or child are defeated by the spirits [of the basilisk] and give up; no longer able to nourish themselves with an external force, they pass out. This is especially the case with old women who no longer have their menstruations and therefore have nauseating exhalations from their mouths and eyes; it is in this way that, looking into a mirror they fog it, because the coolness of the mirror is wrapped in a strong mist [of breath], just as happens with [cold] marble when it is wrapped in a hot southern wind, creating a condensation on its coldness and hardness. And a string touched by their spit becomes putrid; for this reason, sleeping with old women causes children to lose life, while it strengthens the life of the old women.[2]

---

2. *Del senso delle cose e della magia*, Book IV, ch. 14. Cf. Bruno ([1590] 1998), *De Magia*, XLI (p.447 of Tocco's edition of the Italian works): "*Per visum etiam vincitur spiritus, ut passim superius est attactum, dum formae aliter atque aliter ante oculos observantur. Hinc fascinationis activae et passivae ab oculis profiscuntur et per oculis ingrediuntur; unde illud 'nescio ques oculis teneros mihi fascinate agnos.*'" ["The spirit is vanquished through the gaze, as suggested elsewhere (in this text), while the forms are in one way or another before observing eyes. Thus active and passive binding begin with the eyes and enter through the eyes; it is here that we find the origin of: 'I do not know who binds my tender lambs with his eyes.'"] I thank Angelo Tataranno

In the first part of this passage we find neither demons nor witches but only the powers of the soul and psychological relations, but then ambivalent occult natural actions and ancient superstitions of the lowest ceremonial magic reappear. Considered in isolation, these elements are certainly contradictory and unable to be reduced to a logical coherence, but in the concrete context in which they are inserted, they participate in the fundamental unity of tone and inspiration of Campanella's work, entirely permeated by the rediscovery of the power of man at the center of cosmic feeling and suffering. In this passage, therefore, the emphasis is shifted to the psychological interpretation of binding, and the occult actions of a cosmological imaginary—like the ancient superstitions regarding witchcraft—already hint at a retreat into the shadows. Even so, the conscious alternative between magic and rationality does not belong to the "natural magic" of the Renaissance, but rather to the subsequent age of the Enlightenment. Indeed, on the threshold of the Enlightenment we find in Francis Bacon, pioneer of the new epoch, the complete secularization of "binding" and "bewitching," which are understood to be mere psychological relationships:

> There be none of the affections, which have been noted to fascinate or bewitch, but love and envy. They both have vehement wishes; they frame themselves readily into imaginations and suggestions; and they come easily into the eye, especially upon the present of the objects; which are the points that conduce to fascination.[3]

It was the romantic sensibility that brought a decisive contribution to the process of humanization and secularization that placed binding within the circle of human passions and left expressions in our usage of language like "the fascination of personality," "the fascination of a beautiful woman," "bewitching eyes," and so on. Byronic-type heroes, whose "satanism" appeared as an introjection and psychologization of Satan,

---

for his assistance; he notes a syntactical error in the Latin that may have been due to de Martino's transcription. —Trans.]

3. Bacon, *De Invidia*. [The English version here comes from http://oregonstate.edu/instruct/phl302/texts/bacon/bacon_essays.html, accessed April 19, 2014. —Trans.]

dominated the first half of literary romanticism. Let us recall the famous stanzas of *Lara* (Canto 1, xvii–xix), in which Byron draws a melancholy portrait of himself:

> With all that chilling mystery of mien,
> And seeming gladness to remain unseen,
> He had (if 'twere not nature's boon) an art
> Of fixing memory on another's heart:
> It was not love, perchance, nor hate, nor aught
> That words can image to express the thought;
> But they who saw him did not see in vain,
> And once beheld, would ask of him again:
> And those to whom he spake remember'd well,
> And on the words, however light, would dwell.
> None knew nor how, nor why, but he entwined
> Himself perforce around the hearer's mind;
> There he was stamp'd, in liking, or in hate,
> If greeted once; however brief the date
> That friendship, pity, or aversion knew,
> Still there within the inmost thought he grew.
> You could not penetrate his soul, but found
> Despite your wonder, to your own he wound.
> His presence haunted still; and from the breast
> He forced an all-unwilling interest;
> Vain was the struggle in that mental net,
> His spirit seem'd to dare you to forget!

We find analogous features in *The Corsair* and in *The Giaour*. The Corsair is a pallid hero with a high forehead, immersed in a sinister calm that a rapid change in his face's color betrays as a being just a sort of sepulchral stone behind which a world of inchoate mortal passions stirred:

> Too close enquiry his stern glance would quell.
> There breathe but few whose aspect might defy
> The full encounter of his searching eye; […]
> There was a laughing devil in his sneer,
> That raised emotions both of rage and fear;

And where his frown of hatred darkly fell,
Hope withering fled—and Mercy sighed farewell!

The Giaour treats the same theme:

Dark and unearthly is the scowl
That glares beneath his dusky cowl:
The flash of that dilating eye
Reveals too much of times gone by;
Though varying, indistinct its hue,
Oft will his glance the gazer rue,
For in it lurks that nameless spell,
Which speaks, itself unspeakable,
A spirit yet unquelled and high,
That claims and keeps ascendency;
And like the bird whose pinions quake,
But cannot fly the gazing snake,
Will others quail beneath his look,
Nor 'scape the glance they scarce can brook.
From him the half-affrighted friar
When met alone would fain retire,
As if that eye and bitter smile
Transferred to others fear and guile:
Not oft to smile descendeth he,
And when he doth 'tis sad to see
That he but mocks at misery.
How that pale lip will curl and quiver!
Then fix once more as if forever;
As if his sorrow or disdain
Forbade him e'er to smile again.
Well were it so—such ghastly mirth
From joyaunce ne'er derived its birth.
But sadder still it were to trace
What once were feelings in that face:
Time hath not yet the features fixed,
But brighter traits with evil mixed;
And there are hues not always faded,

Which speak a mind not all degraded
Even by the crimes through which it waded:
The common crowd but see the gloom
Of wayward deeds, and fitting doom;
The close observer can espy
A noble soul, and lineage high:
Alas! though both bestowed in vain,
Which grief could change, and guilt could stain,
It was no vulgar tenement
To which such lofty gifts were lent,
And still with little less than dread
On such the sight is riveted.

A pale face, inaccessibility, an apparent calm tainted by the obscure pressure of sinister passions; a melancholy due to mysterious, ancient crimes or to unatoned tragedies; unknown origins and the high lineage of a fallen angel; unbounded pride and the gloomy jealousy of the living: these are all the salient features of the Byronic hero. The "fascination" of this hero lies in the fact that others feel irresistibly acted upon by him, and they become snagged in the weave of a net from which they seek in vain to extricate themselves. The Byronic hero threatens the personal autonomy of decision and choice; he "increasingly occupies thought" and attracts interest with a peremptoriness that challenges the freedom to forget. The servile attitude that his face and bearing provoke in others and the sense of subjection and domination that his gaze generates in its victim have an evil character precisely because they expose the victim to the persistent temptation of being absorbed into his unconscious and thereby become the wretched prey of that unbounded jealousy of the living that ceaselessly wracks the satanic hero. It is not difficult to recognize here an echo of the ancient binding: but now the accent is no longer on the mythic-ritual order of the demonic forces and the ritual of exorcism, and we only have a literary objectification of the heroes and the victims in which Satan becomes the symbol of man's dark side. In the place of myths and rituals, we have here the new romantic sensibility for the intricate *human* relationship between light and shadow, value and passion, consciousness and the unconscious, and out of this sensibility emerge certain figures of poetic fantasy or various literate elaborations. Such a process of humanization and secularization of ancient binding is carried out, moreover, through an emphasis on the very profane world of eros as the elective sphere of evil-doing. The fatal heroes of romantic literature sow the seeds of their curse around them, a curse that weighs above all upon their fate as lovers, in that they consume their beloved women to death. On the model of his private relationship with Augusta or Anna-bella, Byron has Manfred say of Astarte: "I loved her, and destroy'd her!" (*Manfred*, Act II, scene 1 and 2). The fatal Byronic hero as a type cor-responds to the femme fatale, who echoes motifs of ceremonial magic's witches. Just like the hero from one of the ballades of Mérimée's *Gu-zla* who has double pupils—a traditional mark of witches—so, too, does Nyssia, the heroine of Théophile Gautier's *Roi Candaule*. Lewis's Matel-da, Chateaubriand's Velleda, Flaubert's Salammbô, Mérimée's Carmen, Sue's Cécily, and Pierre Louÿs's Conchita are all patently witches or sorceresses who enchant their men to death. Yet they are witches and sorceresses who recite their spells only in the fantasy of literary men, and actually they mediate an experience that is all too profane of what is human (or inhumane) connected to binding, spells, or the power of subjugation and perdition that the femme fatale emanates.[4]

Let us now turn to Southern Italian thought and ask to what extent it participated in this particular process of humanistic resolution with-in the framework of the magic-rationality opposition that had such great importance in the development of modern civilization. Here it is necessary to recognize that during the Renaissance, Southern thought contributed in a decisive way to that process, just as—in general—in certain respects it had a hegemonic function with regard to the choice between demonological magic and natural magic. Southern men in Southern Italy were the ones who yielded the most representative way of dealing with the opposing terms of an alternative that was engag-ing European cultural consciousness, between binding lowered to a vile pact with the devil and binding reabsorbed in the power of human passion and imagination, in a cosmic scenario itself vibrating with hid-den powers and possibilities. Thus the demonological emphasis of *De Fascino* by Vairo from Benevento corresponded to the natural-magic

---

4. For documentation and related issues, see Praz (1942): "La bellezza medu-sea"; and II: "Le metamorfosi di Satana."

interpretation by Bruno from Nola and especially that of Campanella from Stilo. But with the decline of the Renaissance and the advent of the subsequent Enlightenment, and with the reappearance of the magic-rationality antithesis in more rigorous and proper terms, a singular phenomenon developed in Southern thought, one that deserves to be analyzed.

It is already well known that the gradual assimilation of the Anglo-Franco Enlightenment began in Naples in the second half of the 1600s, when a group of philosophers, mathematicians, naturalists, and jurists introduced Galileo, Bacon, Gassendi, and Descartes, initiating a period that had its peak in the subsequent century and that led to the development of works that had European-wide importance. This was a period, moreover, that in Tanucci's time translated into concrete reforms and that—to stick to our subject—led to significant advances in the field of legislation and judicial practice, ending the prosecution of supposed crimes of witchcraft and sorcery. This movement had connections with the polemic against witchcraft and demonology that Giambattista della Porta already begun in the second half of the 1500s, and thanks to it, revivals of superstition—especially during the plague of 1656—were not so widely shared by all social classes as they were in Milan's plague of 1630. On this and on similar occasions, Naples undoubtedly had plebian excesses against that particular type of "binder" known as "dust spreaders," not unlike the Milanese *untori* [plague-spreaders], and it is also true that a part of the Neapolitan nobility joined various scoundrels, prostitutes, priests, and monks in a common superstitious belief in "manufactured" plague. In fact the Duke of Diano, Carlo Calà, attempted in a volume to imitate the ponderings of Father Athanasius Kircher on the "artificial and magic" plague "procured through diabolic arts." A few years before 1656, however, the mathematician, philosopher, naturalist, and doctor Tommaso Cornelio of Rovito parodied this belief, and the doctor Geronimo Gatta similarly deprecated it. When the epidemic of 1656 broke out, the priestly-folk superstition regarding dust spreaders had no credibility with the Health Deputation nor among magistrates and lawyers. That is, at least it did not give rise to trials and convictions, except for the case of one Vittorio Angelucci, a Roman who was indicated by the plebes as the spreader of the aforementioned dusts: he was not convicted for magical arts but rather for actual crimes for which he was found guilty.[5] It is all the more worthy of note that around the end of the century that followed, among circles of people who were not ignorant and in any case were won over to the Enlightenment movement, a sort of dry run to the subject of jettatura developed and spread, and consequently gave rise to a new formation in mentality and custom. This was a period in which the Enlightenment movement had already produced its finest results, and the voices of a Giannone, a Genovesi, and a Filangieri resonated throughout Europe; the solitary Vico had on his own surpassed Enlightenment reason itself and had risen to the concept of an imminent providence in human history. It was Nicola Valletta, disciple of Genovesi and Giuseppe Pasquale Cirillo, doctor *in utroque*, instructor of civil law at the university, who inaugurated this secondary and minor development within the wider Enlightenment. For the "amusement" of the learned brigade that would meet in the home of the upstanding judge Marquis of Villarosa, in 1787 Valletta wrote and published *Cicalata sul fascino, volgarmente detto jettatura*. While, as demonstrated above, the subject of binding had been dealt with in all seriousness by the demonological tradition represented by a Vairo, as well as by the natural magic of a della Porta, a Bruno, or a Campanella, in the *Cicalata* it was dealt with for the first time with a quite particular tone, midway between the serious and the facetious. He chose a suitable literary form for this purpose, not that of the solemn treatise or an engaged discourse, but—precisely—that of the *cicalata*,[6] which as Croce reminds us, is "the prose descendent of the Bernaise poetry lauding unlaudable

---

5. For seventeenth-century Neapolitan culture in general, I refer to what Croce has written in *Storia del Regno di Napoli*, and at greater length, in *Storia* (1932). In Milan in the same period, the situation was certainly worse since the new culture penetrated much later there, and magic and witchcraft formed not only the plebes' belief, but also—and broadly—that of the cultured population (consider Manzoni's Don Ferrante). Even the Court of Health shared the conviction that there were plague-spreaders who had to be hunted and regularly convicted, in order to silence someone like Federico Borromeo (on the different reaction of Naples and Milan to the ideology of magically caused plague, see Niccolini [1937: 196ff.]).

6. The *cicalata* was a literary genre among Italian intellectuals of the seventeenth and eighteenth centuries, a long-winded discourse on something bizarre and patently of little importance. —Trans.

things and asserting untrue truths." Apart from the tone of the dedication to Monsignor Antonio Gürtler, Bishop of Thiene and the Queen's confessor, Valletta speaks explicitly of a "joking subject." In the preface that follows the dedication, he accordingly asserts that in writing this little work, he was pleased to "give body to a shadow and create something from nothing, for the amusement of a learned brigade," the latter being the visitors of the literary meetings in the home of the Marquis of Villarosa. On this basis, it seemed to Croce that the author believed in jettatura only as a literary fiction, and that with this little work he basically indulged a whim or a fashion of the period's high society, that he had become interested in the topic "to have it become something to fill his idleness, a conventional excitation for something about which deep down he did not care and in which he did not believe." Croce recognized that the author "appears to believe firmly in the reality of the object he is treating," but he warns that this appearance was in line with the institution of the chosen literary genre, and thus confirmed that his discourse had the nature "of a misbeliever's joke, or at most of someone who does not believe but nonetheless thinks together with Hamlet that between heaven and earth there are many things that do not enter in our philosophy" (Croce 1945: 20ff.). In my own view, however, this is not exactly how things stand, and Croce's interpretation needs to be corrected.

First of all, we should note that Valletta believed in jettatura, and this belief was not hidden in remote corners of his spirit, as we see from two episodes of his life that he himself narrates. The first episode was when his infant daughter died because a jettatore had looked at her "with a surly and oblique eye." In the second instance, another jettatore made him fail in his attempt to present a petition to the king to ask for dispensation from daily lessons at the university due to his health. But let us listen to his own words:

> I likewise leave aside all observations I have made on jettatura through my personal suffering, oh, how many! oh, what they are! but I cover them beneath ashes of silence, because it should not be said that I be mistaken due to a blind passion for the cause, that I am thought to be deceived or presumed to deceive. I cannot avoid recalling two of the latest jettature, however. The first, my infant daughter, as soon as an impious jettatore aimed at her with a surly and oblique eye, exchanged a most flourishing

life with death. The other: not having recovered, I composed a petition to my most beloved Sovereign, with which I expressed the efforts made over twenty years as Professor of Laws in the University of Regi Studi, and my poor health, which no longer allowed me to do lessons daily: and so I asked what others before me, occupying my same chair, obtained through sovereign munificence. What, then! An intimate friend, whom I later found out to be a terrible jettatore, approached with a burnished appearance; hearing of my claim, as I was about to place myself in the carriage to head to the Royal Villa of Caserta, he replied, "It is difficult." And what came of it? As bad as anything one can imagine in a journey. Flooding waters on the roads, a drunken coachman, an aching horse; as I was finally about to approach the King and humbly present my supplications, I could no longer find in my pocket the petition, which I had until then jealously guarded. The worse thing is that to this day that cursed jettatore recalls that event laughing, retracing my hopes and dashing them. (Valletta 1787: 58ff.)

Croce admits that the mention of these two episodes seems to contradict the interpretation of a belief feigned as a simple literary device. Yet he overcomes this difficulty by asserting that the mention of the baby girl's death "perhaps" constitutes an inappropriate and strident note within the overall tone of the *Cicalata* and its corresponding task of playful literary fiction. It seems to me, instead, that the truth lies elsewhere: that is, Valletta attributed in all seriousness both the death of his little girl and the failure of his journey to the palace of Caserta to the power of jettatura, in the same way that he had to believe in various occult interventions of this sort on several other occasions during his life.

We now need to define how we should properly understand the tone of the *Cicalata* and the spirit with which it was written. After having reflected on jettatura and the firm belief in binding held in the ancient world and the Middle Ages, Valletta reaches Naples of his own time:

But why should I go through dredging up old examples, and why should I abuse your attention transporting you in so many places, through so many periods: as if we did not continuously observe baleful cases of jettatura upon us and others at home, in the square, in the tribunal, in the countryside? I also leave aside innumerable events not thought of, which are however known in our land to men of sincere faith: there, a porcelain box fell from the hands of a renown Councilor, because this man was just as much a jettatore as he was learned—he had only just asked the price of the box and praised it; elsewhere an extremely hard stone for preparing chocolate broke, at the moment that this same jettatore had asked how long it had lasted; here a cat fell from on high on the neck of a heavyset monk, making a pretty picture of him with its claws, just as he was praising it; there golden fruits fell one by one at the appearance of a woman; all of the innocent little birds of a gentleman died, because an evil eye wanted to see them; upon the arrival of a jettatore, the luck of a game changed; misfortunes, storms, aches, dangers, teeth falling out, broken shards, dead horses, dried-up fountains, and innumerable other facts of an all-powerful jettatura. I do not know of which to speak and of which to keep silent. (Valletta 1787: 56)

Here a smile, or—if one prefers—the laugh that this intentionally overdrawn enumeration intends to provoke entails above all a contrast. This is a contrast between a superior cultural consciousness that has learned the great Enlightenment theme of the universe's rationality and the transforming power of human activity illuminated by the light of reason, and an inferior cultural consciousness not yet left behind, according to which, to the contrary, everything goes wrong with a regularity and predictability that form exactly the reverse of the "enlightened" world. This is a reverse to such a degree that not only the victims but the agents themselves—the jettatori—are caught within the weave of this antihuman and antisocial mechanism, and more than agents—which the magicians and bewitching persons of ancient times were, who allowed for making a pact with the devil—they instead tend to be unaware instruments and almost passive breeding grounds for jettatura's sinister power. Second, the tone of the *Cicalata* develops from the lack of a solution to this contrast and from the institution of a psychological and practical attitude of compromise. On the one hand this attitude does not know how to give up the previous ideological engagement, and on the other, in the name of the new Enlightenment arguments, it belittles it to the inferior status of the "joking subject" and the "giving substance to a shadow." But in paying tribute to its own epoch, the work maintains the point and satisfies a need that is present deep down in the soul.

Thus what we have here is not a literary fiction that preserves what is no longer believed at the level of a frivolous joke, but rather a psychological expedient that, in a period no longer suited to treating certain subjects as serious things, feigns to oneself and to others to treat them jokingly, allowing in this way to not give completely up on an ideology and a behavior in which, "deep down," one still believes. A clear-cut detachment separates this attitude from the irony of a Voltaire, who instead underlines a clear choice in favor of rationalism against the "impostures" of superstition and fanaticism. In Valletta there is play instead of real irony, and he makes us smile not so much to bury the cultural past as to indulgently preserve it, veiled by a facetious tone that at times passes into a rascal's clowning: "Does jettatura really exist, you will ask? Look, it has to exist, one replies to another who was performing an enema at night and said that he couldn't find the hole." Back in 1745, in chapter X of his *Della forza della fantasia umana*, Muratori argued against magic and witchcraft and other opinions "so discredited today that they no longer exist except among rough people who are easily taken in and believe in them." With reference to binding he observed, "it would be too unfortunate if humankind were in the hand of others who, through mere will and the glances alone, poisoned those who are healthy." It is precisely a choice of this type, engaged and serious, that is lacking in Valletta. On the contrary, if only on the level of a polemical joke, Valletta momentarily indulges the opposite choice to that made by the Enlightenment, and he hopes for a "science" that in better regulated states would open a school with the aim of teaching men of all walks of life how to recognize and escape from jettatori, rather than "making new systems and ruining man and the world in order to reform it." This amounts to the recognition of a fundamental, unmodifiable irrationality in the course of things human, to the point of making fun of the confident enthusiasm of the period of reforms and of exhibiting the science of jettatura as the only valid and useful one. With his usual ambivalent joking tone, in another passage of the *Cicalata* Valletta requests that human ingenuity finally be applied to the subject of jettatura:

> Lazy and slothful souls, get to work: studying jettatura will allow you to make fantastic discoveries to the benefit of men and nations. If each of us just stood there and did nothing, today we would still believe the

world to be as flat as a table, the sky solid as a crystal, the colors a mix of lights and shadows; we would not travel the seas with fierce and daring helmsmen, the beauty of the skies would not be closer to our eyes, man's gaze would not have penetrated the earth's bowels, and in the breast of divinity, word and the fugacious and flowing sound would not be fixed on paper and with print; and all else accomplished through the ingenuity of man, for whom nothing is impossible when he wills it. You have been negligent and indolent in regard to jettatura, and then you come and deny it to me with a marmoreal forehead and admit it only in the imaginary spaces of fantasy. As for the others, I take an intimate pleasure in the fact that in our times it is not only the low plebes who flee from people who bring misfortune, but also ponderous judges, ranking knights, lawyers, jurists, skilled doctors, sublime mathematicians, keen philosophers, and many cultured and erudite persons known to me. Glory to our century, in which the light of science and fine arts shines clearly and on high; even in this it outdoes the wonderful age of Augustus, when unlucky portents were generally spoken of as what we call jettatura today. (Valletta 1787: 69ff.)

There is a clowning challenge posed here to Enlightenment reason: with an air that stands midway between a rascal's impudence and the flaunted assuredness of an exaggerated Enlightenment man, Valletta claims the rights of the "blind religion" of jettatura. To the devotees of reason scattered throughout Europe, he seems to contrast the "very cultured and erudite" persons of his Naples who, despite their enlightenment, continue to harbor that one area of shadow in their souls: jettatura. In order to better grasp the tone of the *Cicalata* and to distinguish it from the caustic criticism of superstitions coming from Enlightenment thought, it would be helpful to recall the subtle and witty prose with which Manzoni sympathetically judges—employing the literary game of anonymous opinion—the passion of Don Ferrante for treatises of natural magic, and especially that of ritual magic and witchcraft.

Don Ferrante had gone rather more deeply into the secrets of magic and witchcraft, which, as our anonymous author remarks, is a science at once more fashionable and more necessary, and one of which the effects are of far greater importance, and nearer at hand, so that they can easily be verified. We need hardly add that Don Ferrante's sole object in undertaking this line of study was to increase his knowledge and learn all about the evil arts of witches, so that he could ward them off and protect himself from them. With the help, above all, of the great Martino Delrio (the leading authority in this field), he could talk most magisterially about the casting of love spells, sleeping spells, and injurious spells, with the countless variations of those principal types of witchcraft, which, alas, to quote our anonymous author once more, are still to be seen at work every day with such tragic effects.[7]

In a certain sense something of Manzoni's Don Ferrante is still alive in an immediate way in Valletta. What for Manzoni stood as a character that he objectivized and made fun of, in Valetta still operated as part of his personality, though his superior Enlightenment consciousness allowed this part to manifest itself, as already noted, only through a veil of joking.

With this hermeneutic criterion we may evaluate another passage from the *Cicalata*, in which jettatura—"a notion," the author says emphatically, "that has been with us since the beginning of time"—takes on imagined proportions of an occult and perverse cosmic power placed at the disposition of certain individuals without the conscious participation of their will:

Jettatura does not respect powerful men, noblemen, or magistrates, and it dares to advance as far as the high palaces, and it only rejoices and feeds upon the misfortunes of others. By obtaining a chair, a jettatore could well ruin an entire university; a jettatore magistrate can mislead the whole collegial tribunal, to the point that the scale of justice is no longer visible. In the political theater, jettatura can run amok: to be an obstacle to domestic and foreign commerce; to weaken a well-disciplined army; make someone lose his orientation in great matters; reduce an eloquent orator to silence or to chatter; impede treaties between sovereign states. What can this powerful, occult force not do? It counts among the infinite miseries of Nations, it must have been the cause of Darius' defeat:

---

7. Alessandro Manzoni, *The Betrothed* (1827); the citation is from Bruce Penman's English translation (1972: 504–5).—Trans.

it was the oppression of Hannibal, the blood spilled in Cannae, and the shameful humiliation of the Romans to the Samnites' happy self-deception. (Valletta 1787: 140ff.)

Here is the typical physiognomy of the jettatore, which Valletta must certainly have derived from folk tradition, but he gave it new vigor and color, casting the turn of his discourse in an intentionally grotesque color. This confirms his distance from the somber ideology of binding during the Middle Ages and the subsequent epoch of the witch trials:

Certain hulks with their mean faces; certain masks, figures recalling drums and latrines; certain women who, having seen more than one jubilee, cure people of their temptations; some four-day-old larvae—you don't know if they are substance or accident; some scrawny men, more pallid than the poets Philetas and Archestratus, are they not inevitably jettatori? And do they not demonstrate the vices of their souls in their visages? (ibid.: 99)

And nonetheless the author sketches these figures of jettatori with a smile that has something ambiguous about it, and that in fact seems to fade from his lips when he narrates the aforementioned episode of the death of his baby daughter caused by a jettatore. From this we would say that the grim medieval binding returns for a moment to its full legitimacy, breaking with the calculated equilibrium of the work. But only for a moment, because the tone of the *Cicalata* is what it is, and on the whole it remains rather loyal to the rules of the game. Additionally, even in a joking guise, we can perceive in the *Cicalata* something of a voiceless spleen against the tribe of jettatori, a last residue of the fanatic hatred of the preceding age only just left behind. This little work closes with a "project" that clownishly proposes a prize of ten or twenty ecus to the person who figures out how to solve questions like these: whether men are more often jettatori than women, or vice-versa; if people who wear glasses are more likely to be them; if monks are more likely, and if so, monks of which order; if the force of jettatura tends to operate sideways to, in front of, or behind the victim; and so forth. Valletta ends the proposal with a request for a catalogue "of all of the proven jettatori of the City and Kingdom of Naples," in order to be able to defend oneself.

We seem to be reading a parody of the juridical and procedural acumen that we find in instruction manuals for inquisitors called to decide on crimes of magic. Valletta's parody, however, is not entirely innocent, and we notice that the fear and acrimony are only concealed and softened, in keeping with the new times. The parody therefore turns out ambiguous, or at least it loses the innocent and joking quality we would be tempted to recognize in it.

But the point on which we ought to insist is another. The *Cicalata* is usually considered a minor literary product of late seventeenth-century Neapolitan literature, a mere curiosity that had considerable success due to a whim of fashion and the assiduous attention of foreign visitors. If it were only this, given the literary thinness of the work and its extreme theoretical weakness, dwelling on it at length would be the sign of an unproductive mind. One might say that from a literary point of view the *Cicalata* is at most a good read with relatively well-structured erudition, and that from a theoretical point of view it is nonsense; that to deal with the problem of accident and fate seriously and to indicate the limits of abstract Enlightenment reason, *solitary* Vico had already taken the lead, with other means at hand. Vico, whose own life was afflicted by continual ordeals and oppressed in a Neapolitan way by the restrictedness of family life ("the wives who birth babies" and the "children who languish with disease"), elevated himself with authentic mental heroism through the idea of tribulations that can become opportunities and of a providence that is the immanent mind in the course of human history. Yet we must observe that the *Cicalata* is neither thin from a literary point of view nor theoretically nonsensical, but is rather a testament to the history of custom of no small importance. The principal character of this little work, the one for which it merits careful consideration, is that it constitutes a salient document, and in a certain sense an inaugural one, of a new tradition that spread first within the cultured center of Naples in the 1700s, winning over other social strata, and then spread outside of Naples throughout Southern Italy, and with lesser intensity to the North of the peninsula. There is a mood between serious and facetious with which even today many Italians, especially Southerners, often face the theme of jettatura: the "it's not true, but I believe it" (or "I don't believe it, but it's true") with which they bail themselves out of a subject like this; they laugh at the superstitious imagination of jettatura and at the same time indulge in the "you never know" of touching horns or keys—or something else still, which I will leave discretely in my pen[8]: all this developed in Naples in the second half of the 1700s and was set down as tradition in the *Cicalata*. A similar spirit certainly already existed in the cultured stratum of Naples of the period and among brigades of learned men of the sort who met in the home of the Marquis Villarosa. The little poem on jettatura by the man of letters Cataldo Carducci is sufficient to prove this; this poem stimulated Valletta in writing his *Cicalata*, and it deals with the subject with the same tone between seriousness and facetiousness. In the same period, the Latinist and poet from Benevento, Abbot Filippo de Martino, wrote a Latin funeral oration on the occasion of the death of President Genisi's parrot, a parrot that, Valetta states, died "due exclusively to a jettatura caused by a somber and learned magistrate." Filippo de Martino himself wrote the translation in Neapolitan dialect, in which the fatal outcome of the jettatura's effect is sculpted in verse: "*Contr'a chill'uocchie non balette nciarmo*" ("against such eyes could no spell stand"). In this period, too, Giuseppe Pasquale Cirillo, jurist and lawyer, Valletta's mentor, composed the comedy *I Malocchi* and had it performed in his own home. Although he never appeared, the figure of a terrible jettatore, Don Paolo Verdicchio, dominated the scene: his jettatura was so powerful, he could operate at a distance, climbing the bell tower of some church in Salerno and looking toward Naples "with the intention of doing evil."[9] Although the evil eye that appears here is not wholly involuntary and preserves something of ancient witchcraft's spells, the entire episode is presented with an attitude that is similar to the one we have already encountered in the *Cicalata*. Even so, despite such precedents it was Valletta's work that, because of its colloquial and clearly reasoned character, and the liveliness and relative exhaustiveness with which he treats the subject, had the function of *fixing* a vague and fluid attitude circulating in cultured Naples of the period, transforming it into tradition bearing a stability and structural equilibrium, and thus one tending to be spread and shared. In the Neapolitan setting it was Valletta's

---

8.   Here de Martino refers to the apotropaic custom of men touching their testicles. —Trans.

9.   Croce, *I teatri di Napoli*, p. 180. [This citation was incomplete in the original text. —Trans.]

work that advanced the long-begun process of folkloric disintegration of binding as a serious magical belief, be it of ceremonial or natural magic. But at the same time, it was Valletta's book that decisively contributed to stopping the process halfway, in a psychological compromise that was distinctive with respect to the sphere of a differently oriented European Enlightenment "custom." We should now turn to a more thorough evaluation of the *Cicalata*'s cultural efficacy as an instrument of setting down, founding, and spreading the new custom.

Gian Leonardo Marugi of Manduria—a doctor, philosopher, and follower of the progress of science in his period, translator, and annotator of Locke's *Essay*, who in 1797 was called to teach ethics at the University of Naples—was so open to Jacobin ideas, he was given a death sentence during the Bourbon reaction for his active participation in the Parthenopean Republic, but ended up a parliamentarian in 1820. In 1788, the year following the *Cicalata*'s publication, Marugi printed an imitation of the *Cicalata* entitled *Capricci sul fascino*.[10] If we were to evaluate the *Capricci* on the basis of its literary significance or theoretical rigor, we could safely allow it to pass into oblivion: but from the point of view of the history of tradition, this little work instead has a certain importance, and it serves to confirm what has been stated up to this point. In the preface to his *Capricci*, Marugi acts emphatically like a convert after having read the *Cicalata*:

> In my lessons I encountered binding more than once, but since I became acquainted with it as a form without substance, a word without a concept, I hardly paid any attention to it, and in the long run, my ideas of it remained forgotten and neglected ideas. So having nothing in my fantasy but air, wind, fiber, and to my further detriment, intelligent things, perceptions, ideas and a thousand other things that came to that blessed Locke's mind, (upon reading the *Cicalata*) everything appeared new to me, and full of wonder I exclaimed: *tam aperta nescivi!* [I've never seen anything so evident!]. (Marugi 1788, first prose)

At first the author believed that "our actions are the true cause of jettatura," and to obviate jettatura it was enough to "keep to the norm of

---

10. For biographical information, cf. Palumbo (1935).

reason and law," since binding was "vain and chimerical." After reading the *Cicalata*, however, a veil fell from his eyes, and he thanked his friend, who had finally shed light on a series of unfortunate connections and combinations that had taken place in the past and up to then had been without a clear motivation. From now on, he would know the agent that was responsible: jettatura. We might be tempted here to believe that the author abandons himself entirely to irony, with the intention of highlighting the contrast between Enlightenment rationalism and belief in jettatura, thereby playfully reducing such a belief to the absurd. But if that were the case, he would have then needed in his work to remain faithful to this supposed irony and carry out the playful contrast. To the contrary, however, Marugi discusses Valletta's interpretation in complete seriousness, and with a corresponding engagement he proposes new ones. Given this, the passages cited above from the preface appear to be an artifice for moving into the minor sphere of the *capriccio* with the aim of allowing himself a discourse in this sphere that is rather serious: this harks back to the basic tone of the *Cicalata*. Thus the emphasis on Marugi's proclaimed conversion, even if it is not to be taken literally, testifies that the *Cicalata* helped bring to light, shape and set down a need that was in people's hearts, though hidden in their depths. Similar reflections are true of the "comic poem" on jettatura by Baron Michele Zezza (1835), a dialect poet and famous shell sculptor,[11] and of A. Schioppa's *Antidoto al fascino detto volgarmente jettatura* (1832), which in the author's intention was supposed to serve as an appendix to Valletta's *Cicalata*. The traditional ritual gesticulations against jettatura were, as is well known, accurately described by the canonical De Jorio in his *Mimica degli antichi investigate nel gestire napoletano* (1832).

As stated above, what counts in an evaluation of the Neapolitan literature on jettatura is its "tone" and the form of practical coherence of which it is an expression. A Valletta or a Marugi were induced to write their works by an essentially practical stimulus, the practical compromise between old and new beliefs, and not by the need to rethink the Enlightenment option in its theoretical rigor in favor of a world governed

---

11. *La Jettatura poemma cuommeco de lo Barone Michele Zezza* (1835), published by the Società Filomatica ("da li truocchi de la sociatà fremmateca" [the members of the Philomatic Society], as we read on the title page).

by reason, as opposed to a "magical world" of any sort. The *Cicalata* and the *Capricci* were first and foremost facts of custom, and where they have been mistakenly considered as literary or theoretical contributions, they appear woefully lacking. In the *Cicalata* the incoherencies and theoretical oscillations are bountiful: so, for example, while the author sharply rejects every demonological tradition of binding and declares that he wants to keep to the order of "natural" explanations,[12] in point of fact he welcomes some beliefs into his work that come precisely from that tradition, including that of jettatori capable of raising storms. Jettatura is similarly traced at times to the excitement of whims and at other times to material effluvia and emanations that propagate from the fascinating body through vision, words, breath, contact, and the like. Thus a psychological point of view is eclectically mixed with one that is more properly physical-natural and cosmological, along with suggestions from the theories of Mesmer, in vogue in that period. At the same time, Valletta distinguishes between overt and hidden jettatura, the former having recognized causes and the latter not having known causes, and which is connected to the "chain" or "arcane thread" of the universe whereby we give the name of jettatura to those connections that are unfavorable to us and whose dangers are unknown to us. To this Marugi replies that it is better to distinguish jettatura into two large categories of the physical and the moral: the former "attacks the quality of our corporeal substance" and the latter "takes action on willful acts." As he also accepted the tradition of physical jettatura in the form of human power to maliciously provoke winds, storms, lightening, and hail, he even attempted to draw a connection between jettatura and electricity and "explain" the power of jettatori in the meteorological sphere by hypothesizing an electric force emerging from them that charges clouds. It is clear that painstaking investigations and excogitations of this sort are not in and of themselves worthy of discussion. At least in Valletta, however, we find some psychological observations, if occasional and unsystematic, in which a hint of the correct framework flashes. Thus, for example, in discussing the upset

---

12. Valletta protests that he does not want to speak of magic ("God help me! I want to have nothing to do with devils!") and to understand jettatura not as a "diabolical thing" but as a "natural evil influence": cf. Valletta (1787: 5–9).

that a binder induces in his victim's imagination, Valletta illustrates the psychological mechanism in the following way:

> We must thus say that jettatura draws great power from fantasy, and for this reason we sometimes see something that is not there. Therefore if someone has the jettatura power to upset things, whether he communicates his fantasy to us, as Malebranche says, or he is disagreeable to us, we either see things that are not there, or else we see them for what they are and judge them perverse, wrong, and upsetting not only of our little world, but also of operations: these are the most baleful effects of jettatura. When I must do something, should someone approach me whom I understand to be unlucky and jettatore, or who is truly disagreeable to me, with his effluvia against me, fantasy upsets me to the point that I am no longer myself, my inner self, the inner sense and operations of the spirit have no more rule, everything appears evil to me and my very fate appears woeful. . . . The same is to be said if someone, in seeing a twisted hair or another bit of magic, learns of a spell: he already feels the harm. You will say that this is harm from fantasy. But is this not also real and existing? (Valletta 1787: 108)

Here Valletta momentarily touches upon the correct psychological approach that connects the ideology of binding to a real risk of presence, to "no longer being myself," "no longer finding my inner self," and thus to what I have called the experience of *being-acted-upon* that lies at the root of binding and possession and their corresponding protective ideological horizons. In the *Cicalata* it is only a fleeting hint that not only remains without any exploration or development but also without a theoretical connection to other different or contrasting interpretations. This confirms that the unity of the work should be sought elsewhere, on the level of the practical coherence of a formation of ideology and custom that was developing in Naples' cultured circles in the late eighteenth century. The *Cicalata* had a significant impact on this level, and it actually shaped a custom that spread beyond its center of origin. Spreading more widely, the Neapolitan ideology of jettatura, which arose as a compromise between the older binding and eighteenth-century rationalism, was often able to attenuate or lose its original learned grounds, narrowing itself to the "it's not true, but I believe it" of a facetious philosophy, to an observance somewhere between the seriousness and facetiousness of the ritual code illustrated by De Jorio. Moreover, according to the social strata among whom the custom spread, and in relation to the greater or lesser roughness of single individuals, the new custom was able to throw its own compromise off balance by receding to forms that were rather close to the ancient evil binding, earnestly believed in and without the shrewd cultural consciousness of indulging a weakness that was no longer suited to the times. Current folkloric survivals testify to this especially in the peasant world, where binding is simply and obviously an archaic sort of belief (take, for example, the "binding" of envy or the *attaccatura di sangue* and the like in Lucanian folklore). But even with various concrete colorings and nuances, on the whole the new "intonation" of custom made its way, and it widely inspired behavior in Naples and beyond. If we turn to anecdotes of Neapolitan life around the late 1700s and throughout the 1800s, on the subject of jettatura we never encounter characters whom we would define as truly tragic. In contrast, their ancestors of hardly a century or two earlier were tragic, at least in a certain sense: persecuted by popular demand, subjected to torture, condemned in regular trials, and burned at the stake. The narratives regarding Neapolitan jettatori and their victims have reached us wrapped up in a comic atmosphere that arises from the calculated contrast between the consciousness of man as a rational operator lies at the heart of civil living and the scandal of a world in which instead everything goes wrong with predictable regularity only because certain individuals circulate in society who are unaware and involuntary instruments of blind forces that are destructive and perverse. In this regard, the anecdote regarding King Ferdinando I is typical. The King was so convinced that the good De Jorio was a fearful jettatore that for over fifteen years he denied the audience that De Jorio repeatedly requested of him in order to give him the gift of his book. At last, caving in to court pressure, the King received the canonical on January 3, 1825, with the expected result that he died on the morning of the 4th, struck down by a heart attack. As is well known, this anecdote comes from Alexandre Dumas (1889), to whom it was undoubtedly narrated by Fiorentino.[13] It has reached us with a narrative coloring that moves us to laughter, with the good clergyman who

---

13. Cf. *Corricolo* (1889, vol. I: 177ff., Italian translation, 1950: 173). See also Croce, "Il linguaggio dei gesti," in *Varietà di storia letteraria e civile*, pp. 271ff. [This citation is incomplete in the original text. —Trans.]

happily and swiftly approaches his King after a fifteen-year wait, with the intention of handing him the results of his scholarly efforts, without the least suspicion that he is dealing him an unforgiving, mortal blow in that precise moment; and by that extremely rough King, who for fifteen years had defended himself effectively but is unable in the end to avoid making the wrong move that confirms his superstition precisely in the moment in which he unwillingly attempts to get over it. With the same tone and coloring, De Cesare has handed us down anecdotes related to Ferdinando II's belief in jettatura. A great court ball had been set for January 1857, and the Duke of Ascoli had come to the King with the old guest lists in order to proceed with him in a revision of the names, canceling those who were absent, deceased, or politically suspect, and proposing new ones. At one point the Duke of Ascoli suggested the name of Cesare della Valle, Duke of Ventignano, proposing that the King accept his request for an invitation. The King acknowledged the Duke's good qualities and assured political loyalty, but knowing that he had the reputation of a jettatore in the city, said to d'Ascoli: "You know the prejudices that abound on his account; I don't believe it, invite him, but I'm telling you, the ball won't take place." De Cesare himself, in referring the anecdote, does not hesitate to underline the apparent connection between the dreaded jettatura-ridden invitation and what did happen subsequently: the assassination attempt by Agesilao Milano and the ball being canceled. From that time on, moreover, there were no longer any great festivities at court, since the one for the marriage of the crown prince was ruined by the illness and death of the King; during the fifteen months of the Francesco II's reign the ordeals were so many and of such a kind that it was not possible to go beyond the usual receptions, hand-kissing, and circles. Finally, in the last apparent connection with that invitation, the Kingdom itself fell, and the catastrophe was fulfilled. We find an analogous tone in the narrative, again by De Cesare, of Ferdinando II's unfortunate journey on the occasion of the wedding of the Duke of Calabria with Maria Sofia Amalia of Bavaria. As early as the procession of carriages leaving Caserta Palace, upon seeing two Capuchins bent over in bows, after having replied to their salute, the King said to the Queen: "Teresa, what a horrible trip we're going to have this time!" And it was so horrible that it was his last: a snowstorm after the heights of Serra, icy roads, a mile on foot by the already-suffering King in the midst of the blizzard, while peasant mayors and decurions danced about on the snow in order to break it up and prevent the Sovereigns from falling. Then in Brindisi, the first serious attack of his illness, carrying on ill for the rest of the trip, boarding a ship on a litter in Bari to return to Naples by sea, and finally, death. De Cesare tells us that in Ferdinando II, "only the prejudices of jettatura were comparable to his religious fanaticism," and in this regard, "the chronicle records more than a few very salacious anecdotes and good-luck practices that cannot be written in a book, though they are typical and exhilarating." Although he was extremely religious, he held monks and in particular Capuchins to be unlucky, as the episode of the Capuchins of Caserta demonstrates. But on the list of jettatore "types," according to tradition there were also bald men, cross-eyed people, red-haired men, old women with prominent chins, and so on. Ferdinando II's belief in jettatura undoubtedly leaned toward crude popular forms, and with him jokes tended toward a plebian buffoonery and a rascally vulgarity. But when he found himself face to face with death, he dropped the patina of obscene feigning and very nearly brushed up against the ancient drama of dark medieval binding: in the midst of his suffering of his illness he cried out, "They've struck me with jettatura!" He feverishly reviewed the telltale incidents of the fatal trip: the encounter with the two Capuchins of Caserta, certain faces seen in Ariano, in Foggia, in Andria, and finally a bald man who in Brindisi's cathedral had stared at him in an unsettling way and whom he had had removed by Colonel Latour (De Cesare 1908, vol. I: 238, 340ff.).

CHAPTER FOURTEEN

Romantic sensibility, Protestant polemic, and jettatura

Neapolitan jettatura often interested foreign visitors who considered it a specifically local product, although they did not manage to precisely identify—and sometimes they patently misunderstood—its character and coloring as compared with the *mauvais oeil*, the evil eye or the *böse Blick* of their respective nations. These travelers were generally struck by how widespread this belief was in the society, and they inevitably noted that while in their country of origin the cultured strata no longer participated in this "superstition," and a literature on the subject had completely ceased, in Naples all social classes were still engaged in it. Indeed, a university professor, the author of serious treatises of canon and civil law who had participated in the eighteenth-century Enlightenment movement, had published a little book on the topic that enjoyed a widespread popularity among the cultured stratum, and which had multiple editions. The travelers' reaction to jettatura was varied, one of astonishment or laughter, with a frivolous curiosity or humane interest, with pedantic descriptive zeal or to use it as the stimulus for a lively literary rendering of what they had seen and observed. Or they let themselves be overcome by the environment's suggestion and they took on the custom with the zeal and fanaticism suited to neophytes. No matter what their attitude and cultural preparation, these foreign writers in any case lacked a historiographic interest. Mostly literary men and travelers, they abandoned themselves to immediate reactions, and so they could not give the proper importance to precisely the thing that formed the most characteristic feature of Neapolitan jettatura: the cultured combination of skepticism and credulousness, real fear and joking emphasis, conscientious execution of protective ritual and comic ambiguity in gesticulation and facial expression. They were even less capable of tracing the origins of such a particular psychological weaving, which were to be sought—as noted above—in a minor development within the late Neapolitan Enlightenment, and in a practical compromise solution between the old-fashioned witches' binding, the binding of "natural magic," and themes of eighteenth-century rationalism. But even with these limits the foreign literature on jettatura is of interest for the historiographer. Besides some useful data for identifying a certain cultural environment, we find stimulating observations and reflections because the reactions of a foreign traveler indirectly help to better identify particular cultural differences, and because the reactions serve to better illuminate the historical particularities of what elicited them.

In the aforementioned book on Naples, Mayer observed in 1849 that the ideology of jettatura, while widespread throughout Italy, was especially developed in Naples:

> Even the Neapolitans who scorn this belief are not exempt from prejudices on this point, and not infrequently foreigners allow themselves to be influenced by them. In front of a foreigner, men of a certain status readily assume an air of superiority in such matters, and yet when some misfortune suddenly occurs, it becomes evident that this belief is deeply rooted in them. (Mayer 1840: 213ff.)[1]

Here Mayer only just touches upon the characterization of Neapolitan jettatura as a phenomenon that is not only plebian but also cultured, and as an ambiguous compromise between playful skepticism and

---

1. In the original text, de Martino accidently mixed up the Mayer quotation with the one from Dumas' *Le Corricolo* that follows shortly below. I have made the correction here by switching the two quotations. —Trans.

scrupulous credulousness. But the hurriedness of a touristic impression prevents the author from further observation, which remains in part generic and in part equivocal because it lacks a clear identification of the difference between Neapolitan jettatura and binding of more or less immediate origin in witchcraft, without any compromise with the new culture, widespread as it was everywhere and certainly among the Neapolitan plebes of the period. Mayer's observations therefore risk ending up as a mere register of a particular intensity and diffusion of the belief in Naples, without specific qualitative determinations. In Mayer's mind, moreover, the usual judgment of a mere "pagan survival" was solid, including an explicit reference to the antiquity of the belief, to the phalluses and the horn-shaped hands of Pompei's homes and paintings (1840: 215ff.).

It is well known that Dumas dealt with jettatura extensively in his *Corricolo*, published from 1841 to 1843 on the basis of notes taken during his stay in 1835. The first item to note is the importance given to the reaction of a foreigner of the period when, having reached Naples, encounters this singular element of custom:

> When a stranger first arrives at Naples, he laughs at the superstition of the gettatura; then, in a little while, he give the subject more attention, and finally, after a sojourn of about three months, you will see him covered with horns, from head to foot, and his hand eternally doubled. (Dumas 1889, vol. I: 183, Italian translation: 180)[2]

But the reaction of Dumas himself is particularly interesting: he does not participate directly in a custom that is not his own, and he describes its features with a good-natured irony, clearly distinct from the ambiguous attitude of the *Cicalata*:

---

2. Here and elsewhere for Dumas, the English translations are by Roland (1845, *Sketches of Naples*). Roland translates "jettatura" from the French as *gettatura*. Dumas' mention of horns is a reference to the apotropaic use of horn-shaped charms, while the "doubled hand" is the gesture of "making horns" by placing the index and little fingers of the hand out straight, while bending in the middle and ring fingers, touching the thumb. —Trans.

The gettatore is, generally, thin and pale, with a hooked nose, large eyes, which somewhat resemble those of a toad, and which, for the purpose of concealment, he usually covers with a pair of spectacles. The toad, as is well known, has received from nature the fatal gift of the gettatura: he kills the nightingale with his glance. When, therefore, you encounter in the streets of Naples a man of this description, take care of yourself, for there are a hundred chances to one that he is a gettatore. If he is a gettatore, and he first casts a glance upon you, the evil is done; there is no remedy, and you must bow in submission to fate. If, on the contrary, you first get sight of him, make haste to present the little finger extended, and the two others closed; the spell will thus be averted. "Et digitum porrigito medium," says Martial. If, however, you have about you some horns of glass or coral, all these precautions are unnecessary. The talisman is infallible; so, at least, say the vendors. [...] Every time you see two men conversing in the streets of Naples, and one of them keeps his hand doubled behind him in this manner, examine his companion well: he is a gettatore, or, at least, a man who has the misfortune to pass for one. (Dumas 1889, vol. I: 182, Italian translation: 179ff.)

The tone of this prose is free and nonchalant, good-natured, and enlightened, unlike that of the *Cicalata*, thanks to Valletta's effort to define the profile of a custom of compromise in which he directly participated. If anything, in the passage cited here Dumas reminds us somewhat of Manzoni's enlightened irony with regard to Don Ferrante's belief in curses. For Dumas, the magical-religious life of the city of Naples oscillates between the two poles of jettatura and San Gennaro:[3]

The destiny of Naples, like that of all human things, is governed by a double power: it has its bad spirit, which persecutes, and it has its good genius, which protects it; it has its Arimano, who threatens, and its Oromazo, who defends it; its demon, which desires its ruin, and its patron,

---

3. Saint Januarius, the patron saint of Naples. One of the most well-known miracles attributed to San Gennaro is the annual liquefaction of his blood in an anxiously awaited ritual ceremony performed in the Cathedral of Naples. De Martino initiated a research project on the devotion to San Gennaro, but it remained unfinished (cf. Angelini 2008). —Trans.

which hopes to save it. Its enemy is the gettatura; its friend is Saint Gennaro. (Dumas 1889, vol. I: 178, Italian translation: 175)

This observation captures a kernel of truth, except that here, too, we
note a rash generalization of a traveller's "impression": the jettatura-San
Gennaro opposition is only a "connection"—if one of a certain importance—among the many connections and passages that lead from the
crudest forms of ceremonial magic to the most intimate and religiously
open ones.

Even Dumas, like others before and after him, does not have a clear
theoretical distinction between binding and jettatura. Indeed, he recalls
how jettatura is "a plague that the Christians have inherited from the
Gentiles; it is a chain which has passed through all ages, and to which
every century has added a link." In support of this thesis he even attempts an erudite *excursus*, imitating that of the *Cicalata*; indeed, he pil-
lages the data collected by Valletta without any qualms. Nonetheless,
as an insightful writer with a lucky intuition, Dumas actually places a
proper emphasis on a typical feature of the ideology of jettatura: the
anti-Enlightenment theme par excellence of an isolated individual who
unknowingly and unintentionally becomes the blind instrument of an
occult and maleficent force, who systematically introduces disorder into
the natural, social, and moral spheres.

In the Neapolitan ideology of jettatura, as it was described by the
various Vallettas and Marugis, the "unaware maleficent power" that
emerges from certain persons takes on the specific meaning of a sem-
iserious antithesis to human reason as a reformer of natural, social, and
moral order. The jettatore in fact appears to be the man of absolute disorder in these three spheres, and at the same time he is the man of the
occult and the unconscious, who in the century of the lights contradicted
all of the lights of the century, inducing the use of amulets and good-
luck charms as remedies. As Valletta gives us to understand in the passages cited previously, the jettatore is the living irony of an enlightened
reformability and rationality of the world, so that—he says—in place of
reforming systems, we would do better to carefully study jettatura and
open a school for teaching people how to recognize jettatori and protect
themselves from them. Precisely in this connection, the biography that
Dumas sketches of a character whom he calls the Prince de *** is highly

exemplary. In a free literary elaboration, this character condenses some historical details from the life of the fearsome Duke of Ventignano and imaginary elements portrayed according to the tradition of jettatura, and in particular, according to the typology of the *Cicalata* (Dumas 1889, vol. I: 185, Italian translation: 182).[4] The prince's fatal influence played out above all within his family and thus had a range of action that we might call circumscribed. As tradition would have it, the "prince" initiated a series of misfortunes from the time he was born: his mother relinquished her life in the delivery; the nurse to whom he was entrusted lost her milk; his father was removed from his post as ambassador in Tuscany, because at the news of the birth of his son and the death of his wife he abandoned his post without the Sovereign's authorization and hurried to Naples. The prince continued this jettatura action in his domestic circle throughout his entire long life: thus his older brother perished in a duel in order to defend him from the accusation of being a jettatore, and his son-in-law—who as a bachelor had been a libertine—could not consummate his marriage to the prince's daughter due to the effect of the father's blessing bestowed upon the couple. But the prince's baleful activity went well beyond the family circle, and it ranged freely throughout the society. The day the prince entered into the seminary, all of the boys in his class were struck by a convulsive cough. During his studies he surpassed his classmates and always earned the prize, except once when he was second place; but then his classmate who had won the first prize tripped on the first step of the stage when he went to receive his garland and broke a leg. Nor were the monks of Comaldoli monastery safe when the prince entered to become a novitiate, because the day after his entrance the ordinance of the Parthenopean Republic appeared, abolishing religious communities. Having abandoned his plan to devote himself to religious life to instead become wealthy at his brother's expense, he initiated his high-society life, going to San Carlo for the first time: that evening the theater caught on fire. Invited to a party given by a certain countess, everything went wrong: a great storm prevented people from staying in the garden, a chandelier fell, the prima donna of San Carlo sang off-key and abandoned the hall, "feeling that

---

4.   On the Duke of Ventignano see F. Nicolini, "Un jettatore napoletano non ancora eguagliato," in *Giornale*, Naples, November 16, 1947.

she was under the influence of an inauspicious power, superior to her talent," and so on. From the time he was a youth the prince displayed a striking aptitude for operating on a wider, even national, scale. Once, when he was still at the seminary, he was sent as class representative to the Church of Santa Chiara to attend the blessing of the troops who were leaving to fight the French: as soon as the Archbishop gave his blessing and the flags marched to exit the church, one of the standard-bearers dropped dead from a heart attack precisely at the moment in which he passed before the prince. The latter left the line and kneeled over the unlucky wretch, and after attempting in vain to revive him, he pulled the standard from the corpse's contracted hands, raising the cry, "Long live the King!," which was echoed by the crowd. As a result, three months later the Neapolitan army was defeated by the French, and the very standard that his inauspicious hands had touched fell to the hands of the victorious enemy. The prince's power of jettatura subsequently had positive tests on an international level: when he headed to Paris with the mission of complimenting Charles X on behalf of the King of Naples for the capture of Algiers and was solemnly received at court, the next morning the revolution broke out in Paris. On his way home, the prince launched another unconscious strike, heading to Rome to pay homage to Pious VII and kiss his hand devotedly. Three days after that homage and that kiss, the pope went the way of all flesh. Did Valletta not announce, in his grotesque Gospel, that jettatura can "run amok in the political theater?" Last but not least, not even meteorological events were immune to the prince's sinister influence: Dumas dwells at length on the description of an unlucky sea journey, during which the French frigate hosting the prince was forced into a one-sided battle against English ships, as the wind had most inopportunely changed direction as soon as the prince had reassured the captain that it would continue to blow in a favorable direction. In conclusion, in Dumas' fictionalized biography, the Prince de *** appears as the most radical negation of the very possibility of a life in society, and rises to become a living symbol of irrationality, evil, and the unconscious. Even so, nothing in Dumas' biography recalls the figure of a tragic hero: this is in keeping with the spirit of Neapolitan jettatura, which only knows purposefully grotesque heroes, the object of comic terror. But even jettatura—as resistant as it is to a romantic interpretation[5]—had its own adventure in this sense thanks to the work of Théophile Gautier. The protagonist of the story entitled *Jettatura*, the French nobleman Paul d'Aspremont fits in perfectly with the Byronic model of the rebellious and satanic hero:

He was a young fellow of twenty-six to twenty-eight years. At least such was the age one felt tempted to give him at first glance, though when he was examined attentively he seemed to be either younger or older than that, so curiously mingled were weariness and youthfulness upon his enigmatic countenance. His hair, of that dark fairness called auburn by the English, shone in the sunlight with coppery, metallic sheen, and in the shade seemed almost black. His profile was clear cut, his brow would have called forth the admiration of a phrenologist thanks to its protuberances, his nose was nobly aquiline, his lips well formed, and his chin had that powerful roundness that recalls the medals of antiquity. Yet, these various features, individually handsome, did not form an agreeable whole. They lacked the mysterious harmony that softens contours and makes them melt one into another. There is a legend of an Italian painter who, seeking to represent the rebellious archangel, composed a face of dissimilar beauties and thus attained an effect of terror far beyond what is possible by the use of horns, arched eyebrows, and unholy grin. The stranger's face produced a similar impression. His eyes, in particular, were extraordinary. The black lashes that edged them contrasted with the pale gray color of the pupils and the auburn shade of hair; the thinness of the nose caused them to look nearer each other than allowed by the

5. Cione seems to recognize this resistance when, in speaking about folklore and popular literature in Romantic Naples from 1830 to 1848, he observes that while many features of the life and custom of the city were subject to Romantic idolization on the part of foreigners and among the Neapolitans themselves, the ideology of jettatura offered much less appeal to the sensibility of the period (Cione 1942: 316): in fact, in the writings of Zezza, Schioppa, De Jorio, and Bidera, jettatura was basically tied to the framework given to it by Valletta and Marugi. If in other respects these writings fit into the movement of so-called romantic realism, the fundamental sensibility with which the question of jettatura was faced did not constitute anything new with respect to the two eighteenth-century scholars who initiated the discussion.

rules of drawing, and as for their expression it was quite undefinable. When the young man's gaze did not consciously rest upon anything, it was moist with vague melancholy and soft tenderness, but if he looked at anyone or anything, his brows bent, and formed a perpendicular wrinkle on his forehead; the pupils lost their gray color and turned green, spotted with black spots, and striated with yellow lines; his glance then flashed sharply, almost painfully, after which he would resume his former placidity, and from a Mephistophelian individual turn into a young man of the world—member of the Jockey club, if you like—on his way to spend the season in Naples, and glad to step on a lava floor less mobile than the "Leopold's" deck.[6]

In the course of the story, Paul contemplates himself in the mirror in order to discover the inauspicious signs of the jettatore's figure, and he is dismayed to recognize the features of a Medusa-like beauty:

He went to the mirror and looked at himself with terrifying intensity. The dissonant perfection of features, composed of beauties not usually found together, made him more than ever like the fallen archangel and gleamed with sinister fire out of the dark depths of the mirror. The rays in his pupils writhed like vipers; his eyebrows quivered like a bow from which the deadly shaft has just been shot; the white line in his forehead recalled a cicatrice due to a thunderbolt, and the flames of hell seemed to burn in his auburn hair, while the marble pallor of his complexion brought out more startlingly still each feature of his absolutely terrifying face. He was frightened at himself. It seemed to him that his glance, reflected by the mirror, returned to him like a poisoned arrow. Imagine Medusa looking at her own hideous yet charming face in the ruddy reflection of a brazen shield!

A wounded and melancholy beauty, an apparently calm face, an indefinable age and gloomy inaccessibility, a fallen archangel's somber dignity and a gaze that consumes from within the things or the person

---

6.   Citations from Gautier's book are from the English translation available from the Project Gutenberg of Australia: http://gutenberg.net.au/ ebooks06/0605721h.html. —Trans.

upon whom it falls: these are certainly the traits of the Byronic hero. In contrast to this, let us recall the aforementioned passage from the *Cicalata*: "Certain hulks with their mean faces; certain masks, figures recalling drums and latrines; certain women who, having seen more than one jubilee, cure people of their temptations; some four-day-old larvae—you don't know if they are substance or accident; some scrawny men, more pallid than the poets Philetas and Archestratus . . ." All told, one can measure the distance between the works not only on a strictly literary level, but precisely that of "sensitivity" and custom.

The maleficent power of the Byronic hero developed from the romantic idolization of rebellious individuality, from the exaltation of the irrational and the occult against abstract reason, and from the interiorization and humanization of Satan as opposed to his mythological depictions. The Neapolitan jettatore was a modest local formation expressed by a group of Enlightenment thinkers who had not managed to live out the choice between magic and reason in all seriousness, and it was on this particular point that they kept to a compromise between seriousness and facetiousness. We can thus well understand how the two cultural entities were incommensurable, and how the transformation of the jettatore into a fallen archangel could give rise to a hybrid product in which, on the one hand, jettatura got completely misunderstood, and on the other, the Byronic hero took on grotesque and strident notes. Only superficially does Paul d'Aspremont abandon himself to the recurrent exploits in the tradition of jettatura, as when with a simple glance he makes a boat of laborers who approached the *Leopold* overturn from a sudden large wave; or when he goes to the theater, where he disorients the actor playing the part of Pulcinella. These episodes remain extraneous, and their levity does not get confused with the somber connotations of the satanic hero. The episode narrated by Gautier is well known: Paul's love consumes a sensitive English girl, Alicia Ward, and sends her to her death thanks to his maleficent gaze, while a Neapolitan gentleman, Count d'Altavilla, seeks in vain to save Alicia from her fate. Paul discovers that he is a jettatore, and is divided between desperation and jealousy. The bleak and murky drama arrives at an epilogue among the ruins of Pompei, where a savage stiletto duel takes place between the two rivals. But since the gaze of the jettatore would alter the equal conditions of the duelers, the two agree to blindfold their eyes "pour égaliser les chances." Despite this, even through the blindfold Paul's eyes continue to exert their fatal power, and Count d'Altavilla ends up getting himself miserably stabbed on his adversary's stiletto. After having contemplated Alicia for the last time and having absorbed the image of her fragile life, Paul blinds himself with a blazing steel dagger in the desperate attempt to free himself and those around him, above all Alicia, from such a curse. After this, he hurries to his beloved, whom he naturally finds already dead (loved her, and destroy'd her!"), and in the end he throws himself into the sea from a jutting rock.

It would be too easy to insist on the inconsistencies in the aesthetics and taste of this story: what is important to highlight here is the misunderstanding of Neapolitan jettatura, which Gautier attempts to place within the very different model of the satanic hero of the romantic age. Feeling himself pointed to as a jettatore, Paul d'Aspremont remarks that in none of the many European cities he visited had he ever received such a reception, and he marvels at this:

> I do not remember ever having produced such an effect in Paris, London, Vienna, or in any of the towns where I have lived. I have been thought proud, disdainful, reserved at times. I have been told that I affected the English sneer, that I was aping Lord Byron, but everywhere I have been received as a gentleman should be ...

But one day, walking through the Chiaia district, he is forced to escape from the unpleasant attention of the people thronging the streets and he takes refuge in a bookshop where his eye falls upon Valletta's *Cicalata*, which offers him the key to the mystery: if d'Aspremont had come across this book in Paris, he would have glanced carelessly through it as through an old almanac stuffed full of nonsensical tales, and have laughed at the serious manner in which the author treated of such absurdities. But in his present condition away from his usual surroundings, prepared to credulity by numberless trifling incidents, he perused it with secret horror, like some profane person spelling out of a black-letter folio formula for the vocation of spirits and other cabalistic performances. Though he had not sought to penetrate them, the secrets of hell were being revealed to him, and he was now aware of his fatal gift: he was a jettatore!

With regard to the "serious tone" of Valletta, it is clear that we have a basic misinterpretation here: the *Cicalata* is not a book that reveals "the secrets of hell," but merely a playful compromise. The misunderstanding goes so far that Gautier uses jettatura as an excuse for an engaged exaltation of the powers of the irrational and the unconscious, in keeping with romantic fashions. When Paul unexpectedly kills his rival in the blindfolded duel, he protests that he is as innocent as a thunderbolt or an avalanche, "as all destructive, unconscious forces." And further:

> The human mind, even when most enlightened, has always some dark nook in which crouch the hideous monsters of credulity and where cling the bats of superstition. Ordinary life itself is so full of problems that cannot be solved that impossibility becomes probability. A man may deny everything or believe in everything; from a certain point of view dreams are as true as reality.

In order to justify how a worldly young man, imbued with modern science, could persuade himself in Naples to be a jettatore, Gautier employs the following motivation:

> Common belief exercises an irresistible power of magnetism which masters a man in spite of himself, and with which the individual will cannot always cope successfully. A man may arrive in Naples laughing jettatura to scorn, and end by surrounding himself with horned preventives and by fleeing from every individual whose glance he suspects of evil.

Finally, the sweet Alicia—of Protestant faith, a rationalist to the point of not accepting anything without a critical examination, and who only accepted as true what could be mathematically proven—fell miserably victim to Paul's occult influence. Yet Neapolitan jettatura, as the various Vallettas and Marugis defined it, did not at all represent an "engaged" or "serious" choice in favor of the irrational: as a playful local compromise it badly tolerated the weight of complex and passionate romantic oppositions.

We find another form of foreign reaction to jettatura in the Protestant polemic against the superstitions of Southerners. In this regard, the aforementioned work of Trede is no doubt exemplary, dedicating an entire chapter to jettatura (1889–91, vol. II: 226–57), where we read the usual generic statements about the widespread belief in it in Southern Italy and the secret subscription to the superstition in those Neapolitans who say, "I respect jettatura, even if I don't believe in it" (vol. II: 209, 227f., 229). The obtuse anti-Catholic polemic united with an awkward professorial pedantry lies at the foundation of the mistaken evaluation of Neapolitan jettatura as a "science" and of Valletta as the "philosopher of the evil eye." We also find a substantially incorrect fact, in that Valletta is passed off as a "Neapolitan statesman" (Trede 1889–91, vol. II: 210). But the author's professorial clumsiness appears above all in this passage:

> In the course of this exposition, the reader will become acquainted with words and expressions that are entirely unknown in Germany due to their conceptual contents, and for whose translation the entire German vocabulary offers no aid. The word "jettatore" in German would be *Werfer*, and "jettatura," *Das Werfen*: but with these terms the reader will not be able to understand a thing. "Corno" is *Das Horn*, "cornicelli" translates into *Hörnchen*, "fare le corna" is *Das Horn machen*, and "malía," *Das Übel*: but if the reader wants to understand these expressions relative to the chapter here on evil eye, it is necessary to offer some lengthy explanations. (Trede 1889–91, vol. II: 229)

We should observe that the word *jettatura* is certainly untranslatable in German, as in any other foreign language, simply because it designates an ideological formation and a custom that arose in Naples at the end of the eighteenth century. Because Trede has no understanding whatsoever of this historical and local coloring of the word, and he connects its meaning to the traditional bewitching binding, it behooves us to recall that the German language, like any other European language, presents a significant wealth of terms, even local ones, to designate binding, to fascinate, to be fascinated, and so forth.[7]

From this concise analysis of the most important foreign writers on jettatura, we find further confirmation of the thesis argued here. All of these writers more or less perceived that they were dealing with a local custom, though they did not successfully identify its origin and

---

7.   See the list of German terms in Seligmann (1910, vol. I: 50ff.).

character, and they ended up connecting it to its "pagan" antecedents. This explained the local fact of the greater diffusion of the custom in all social strata as compared with other cities in Northern Italy or Europe. Only one foreign author, Dumas, came close in an intuitive way to the character of the Neapolitan jettatore, skillfully sketching the fictionalized biography of the Prince de ***. The fact that jettatura remains substantially resistant to any romantic reformulation indirectly confirms the Enlightenment climate to which its ideology is to be traced. Thus the writer who attempted this sort of reformulation, Gautier, only managed to put together an involuntarily grotesque story, in which we perceive the strident contrast between the two separate cultural orientations, the satanic hero of European romanticism and the much more modest Neapolitan jettatore, with the comic terror that his appearance provokes, and for this its facetious element could never have tolerated the moniker of "fallen archangel."

The limits of the foreign writers on jettatura persisted in the field of studies that are more strictly folkloristic, with the aggravating circumstance that they entirely lost that bit of intuitive insightfulness that fresh impressions of gifted observers would occasionally have in their corresponding literary elaborations. Thus, in 1895, Elsworthy did not hesitate to proclaim Naples "the home par excellence of jettatura" (1895: 18) without, however, clarifying the historical significance of such a preeminence. Similarly, in his erudite ecumenical compendium on the evil eye, Seligmann incorporated jettatura within the immense documentation on binding, understood in its traditional sense.[8]

---

8.   Seligmann (1910, vol. I: 32ff., 191, 216). Cf. Andrews (1897). In general the folkloristic literature either confuses jettatura and evil eye, or else it keeps to the typological classification according to which jettatura is involuntary, whereas evil eye involves a deliberate intention to harm and perhaps the ritual of an actual spell. This literature does not grasp the historical origin and meaning of the Neapolitan ideology of jettatura, nor the historical distinction from ancient and medieval binding, and from the binding of natural magic. See, for example, Wagner (1913: 129ff.); La Sorsa (1915: 49ff.); Palumbo (1935); Bonomo (1953: 19–88). Much the same can be said for the monographs by Tuchmann, Mancini, and Gifford cited in Chapter 11, note 10, p. 116.

Chapter Fifteen

The Kingdom of Naples and jettatura

It still remains to be explained why precisely in Naples around the end of the eighteenth century a particular custom of compromise developed that, by combining the ancient magical binding with Enlightenment rationalism, gave rise to the ideology of jettatura and to the corresponding psychological attitude that accompanied it. Moreover, why was it in Naples, amid the baseness of particularly tenacious folk survivals and the heights of a cultural life oriented in a modern and European sense, that this intermediate formation gradually inserted itself? It was a calculatedly balanced formation somewhere between past and present, between cultured skepticism and plebian credulousness, and between facetious disbelief and ritual scrupulousness. Pondering the naturalistic interpretations of the history of the Kingdom of Naples, which attribute the causes of Southern Italy's misfortunes to the climate or the poverty of the soil or the race, Croce noted that if the elaborators of such interpretations had lived in the eighteenth century, they would have looked to another cause, in keeping with the period's philosophy, such as bad sovereigns, priests or the Spanish. That is, "[i]f . . . they held to the mockingly superstitious beliefs dear to so many Neapolitans, they would blame them on the evil eye, always the nemesis of stable government, as when it rendered sterile the queens of the Normans, the Angevins and the Durazzeschi, and thus paved the way for one war of succession after another."[1]

This "superstitious Neapolitan philosophy," so obviously irrelevant as "philosophy" or even as a criterion of historiographic interpretation, constitutes a particular cultural product as a "custom" in an organic connection with the history of the Kingdom of Naples. It was precisely Croce who, in the very moment he repeated that a history of the Kingdom of Naples could not be reduced to a list of disasters, failures, and catastrophes, nonetheless recognized that it was particularly "thankless" and "difficult" to narrate, unlike "a history of greater importance, with a definite line of development, a beginning, middle, and end, a logic that the mind can follow and understand and depend upon." And admitting that such a difficulty was "intrinsic and effective" (that is, inherent to the material to be treated and not entirely attributable to the historian's possible deficiency), he recalled how the character with which the history of the South immediately presents itself is one of "a history that is no history, a development that does not develop"; whereas the history of other parts of Italy, of Venice, Florence, Genoa, of the communes and seigniories of Lombardy, "is characterized by the impetus of their political bodies, their struggles for liberty and power, their trade and industries, their seafaring prowess and colonies, their poetry and art."[2] And summarily reviewing the noted features of the South's nonhistory, Croce underlined how Southern Italy, apart from a speculative sphere with various Brunos and Campanellas, had participated to an insignificant degree in the second civilization that from the Italian peninsula radiated out to the world: the civilization that rose from the city-states to the full Renaissance. So while Byzantine-Norman-Swabian civilization fell apart and the center of cultural life passed to the city-states, in the South a Kingdom of Naples arose that was without its own principle of inner life and unsupported by the sinew of a social formation dedicated to commerce and industry. On the contrary, it was continuously upset by the quarrelsomeness and particularism of the baronage. The logical outcome of this was the "decline" of the Kingdom and Viceroyalty: another catastrophe,

---

1. Croce. *Storia del regno di Napoli*, pp. 286ff. [English edition translated by Frances Frenaye as *History of the Kingdom of Naples* (1970: 244). —Trans.]
2. Croce (1970, English edition p. 233). —Trans.

although it had its logic in the fact that the independent kingdom did not have the strength to control the barons, whereas the Spanish domination in Southern Italy had had this strength to some extent. In this turbulent history (or, if one prefers, this nonhistory) Croce finally finds a clearly positive moment in the new Enlightenment culture that entered Naples around the mid-1600s and lasted approximately a century and a half. Especially with Giannone and Genovesi, this Enlightenment culture amounted to forming a moral and civil personality in the "Neapolitan nation" for the first time, if only within a very limited circle of learned men. Thus, despite the search for the positive that is connected to every engaged work of historiography, Croce's treatise highlights the extraordinary power of the negative in the history of the South. This is a real power that is manifested in the relative restrictedness of *res gestae* in the economic and political spheres, and therefore in the aforementioned difficulty of writing a corresponding *historia rerum gestarum*. Ancient and modern voices attest to this power, and one counting for the great multitude is that of Campanella. In his proposals for increasing the revenues of the Kingdom of Naples, here is the way in which the philosopher from Stilo gives us insight into the conditions of the provinces in the late sixteenth and early seventeenth centuries:

> Famine thus arises from the negotiating art, since the merchants and powerful usurers purchase all grains from the farmyard, they keep them long enough to leave the people hungry, and then they sell them at triple or quadruple the price. When they do not find so much profit as their greediness yearns for, they keep it for a third, fourth, fifth year or longer, and then they sell it stinking and mixed with other grain, and thus along with hunger they create pestilence. As a result the land depopulates, some flee from the Kingdom, others die from that vile food or are oppressed by usury, hunger, plague, and troubles; many do not take wives so as not to have their children suffer this misery, and the women become whores for a piece of bread. (Amabile 1882, vol. II)

This description corresponds to that of Naples as the antithesis of the City of the Sun, in which goods are not valued because everyone has what he needs and men are without envy, jealousy, and arrogance:

But with us, alas! It is not so. In Naples there exist 70,000 souls; out of these scarcely 10,000 or 15,000 do any work, and they are always lean from overwork and are getting weaker every day. The rest become a prey to idleness, avarice, ill-health, lasciviousness, usury, and other vices, and contaminate and corrupt very many families by holding them in servitude for their own use, by keeping them in poverty and slavishness, and by imparting to them their own vices. Therefore public slavery ruins them: useful works, in the field, in military service, and in arts, except those which are debasing, are not cultivated; the few who do practice them doing so with much aversion.[3]

From an existential point of view, this lasting power of the negative translates into the recurring experience of the precariousness of elementary goods for survival, the insecurity of prospects, the chaos of clashing particularistic and individualistic interests. More generally, it translates into an uninterrupted pressure of uncontrollable forces—be they natural or social—pressing in on all sides and crushing the individual, while culture as a whole or the society in its fabric do not offer the possibility of realistic, efficacious behaviors for dealing with the negative and bringing it down to a human proportion. It is precisely within this context that we must consider the particular importance in the South of the use of protective techniques of low magic, the magical tone of Catholicism, the multiplicity of intermediate magical-religious connections, the broad spirit of compromise, and high culture's scant capacity for expansion. It is here, too, that we place the fact that Southern thought participated in a decisive way in the choice between demonological magic and natural magic, but not in the choice between magic and the science of nature, which in the South remained without significant contributions. When Enlightenment thought, born in the full vigor of the English and French bourgeoisie, reached Naples in the second half of the 1600s, it renewed cultural life. It led to the development of a literature that in the course of the subsequent century rose to a European level, and it of no small importance that here, in Naples, a whole series of conditions made it

---

3. *Città del Sole*, p. 76 [English translation from the version available from the Gutenberg Project, http://www.gutenberg.org/files/2816/2816-h/2816-h.htm, updated January 26, 2013. —Trans.]

impossible to experience an option in favor of rationality which Bacon and Descartes had, each in his own way, experienced.[4] The limit *in re* that the Anglo-French Enlightenment found in Naples was given by the lack of a commercial and industrial bourgeoisie as a vigorous and consolidated economic class on the rise within an expanding nation-state. The rationalism of a *literary* bourgeoisie like that of Naples therefore developed with features in line with these conditions, without the particular engagement and sensibility for the choice between magic and rationality, and superstition and science, that were so important in the development of the Anglo-French Enlightenment. It has been correctly underlined that the Neapolitan Enlightenment thinkers basically kept themselves far afield of any explicit and direct polemic against traditional religion, especially in its most compromised folk forms, limiting themselves in the polemic solely to the political aspect of relations between church and state (Croce 1970: 181ff.).

It is in this overall framework that we must place the formation of the Neapolitan ideology of jettatura as an element of connection and compromise between the bewitching binding of low ceremonial magic and the rational requirements of the century of lights. It was a formation in which, on the level of custom, a contrast surfaced between the Anglo-French Enlightenment and the nonhistory of the Kingdom of Naples, or—more precisely—between a movement of thought that was born and reached maturity in two great national monarchies in the full development of their respective bourgeoisies, and the lack of

---

4. It should be recalled that Bacon's "reform" is comprehensible only within the context of the commercial and political development of Elizabethan England. Paolo Rossi has recently highlighted how one of the fundamental features of this "reform" was the request for a science based on collaborative efforts, regular exchanges, and the public circulation of results: this is precisely what was lacking in "natural magic." Rossi further observes that "when the Encyclopedists addressed themselves to the 'artisans of France' and visited laboratories to question technicians and workers and 'take down their replies,' [and they] tried to find exact definitions for the ends and methods of each separate art so as to compile a complete *corpus* or encyclopedia of learning," they consciously presented themselves as the heirs to the great "reform" begun by Bacon (Rossi 1957: 78ff., English edition Rabinovitch 1968). In Naples, developments of this sort lacked all of the conditions.

these conditions in the Kingdom of Naples, a new area of influence of that movement. The compromise represented by the ideology of jettatura must therefore be considered proof that, all told, the Neapolitan Enlightenment could not experience an important choice in which the Anglo-French Enlightenment was engaged. This occurred because the entire life of Southern society in that period, as it resulted from its history, refused such an experience: the delay in economic and political development, thus the level of a secular employment of man's technical power, rendered the use of ceremonial techniques of the magical moment psychologically current, in a protective function of individual presence forced to maintain itself in a world in which everything "goes wrong."

Up until the fall of the Kingdom and beyond, the ideology of jettatura grafted itself onto public as well as private life in the city of Naples. It is precisely this public reflection that allows us to better understand the connection between the ideology in question and the objective disorder of Neapolitan society. Unlike demonological magic, in which the figure predominated of poor women branded as witches and persecuted as such, jettatura is dominated by characters who are mostly male, very often representatives of the cultivated strata, and by public officials, professors, scholars, doctors, lawyers, and magistrates. As with every form of binding, Neapolitan jettatura undoubtedly tends to get specified and institutionalized in relation to those critical moments that recur in real life, where we usually encounter the frustration of desires and expectations, the uncertainty of prospects, and at the same time, man's impotence in correcting the course of things within the context of a society and culture that do not offer efficacious means for "realistic" struggle. Additionally, Neapolitan jettatura has the specific feature of being a belief that penetrated the life of the tribunal and the palace, taking on a public dimension. I already mentioned the belief in jettatura on the part of Ferdinando I and Ferdinando II, but the form of jettatura that we may call "judicial" merits special mention. It is well known that since the end of the sixteenth century, the bar in Naples thrived on the Kingdom's muddle of rights and the multiple legislations, the great number of disputes that flowed into the capital from all of the provinces, and the spread of a litigious spirit within the general idleness. In this regard, Giannone underlines how in "a kingdom divided by the Spaniards into so many small baronies and new investitures, such a proliferation of barons could only sustain the feudal condition and fill the tribunals with new disputes and questions" (Giannone 1844, ch. 4; cf. De Cesare 1908, vol. I: 350ff.; and Croce 1970: 129ff.). The Holy College in Santa Chiara and the spacious rooms of Castel Capuano thus truly comprised one of the most characteristic expressions of the disorientation, the confusion, the vain thinness, and in the final analysis, the irrational in Neapolitan life. It was thus understandable how the ideology of jettatura enjoyed special favor in an environment of this sort, where a requested or hoped-for outcome depended on a myriad of imponderabilia, and where justice and arbitrariness, law and abuse, were inextricably confused. In his emphatically ambivalent depiction of a world governed by jettatura, Valletta did not neglect to mention the magistrate type of jettatore who enchants and dazzles "the entire collegial tribunal, so that the scale of justice is no longer visible." Here, enchantment and dazzling are not so much a matter of smooth talking or quibbling, as they are an occult psychic power that makes the judges lose any aptitude for discerning true from false and just from unjust. The ideology of judicial jettatura lasted throughout the nineteenth century, and it formed a significant part of what the Neapolitans called "postponing jettatura" with which, generally, one indicated the power of some jettatori to impede the execution of an important operation of the day. In particular, if a certain person was heading to court and met one of these characters that specialized in interrupting and spoiling, it was a sign that the case would be postponed *sine die*.[5] Trede relates an important trial held in Naples in 1887, which could not begin before having satisfied the audience's riotous request to remove a certain person from the courtroom who was a noted perpetrator of postponing jettatura: the mere presence of this person was enough to "mislead the entire collegial tribunal" and have the accused found not guilty, when the audience instead desired his conviction (1889–91, vol. I: 245).

The connection between the objective disorder of social life, the lack of civil ethos, and the ideology of jettatura in concrete Neapolitan life

5. On postponing jettatura in Naples in the second half of the nineteenth century, see Rolfe and Ingleby (1888: 107ff.).

became particularly evident during the events in 1855–56 that led to the planned construction of the Apulian train line. The proponent of the project was the handsome and eloquent engineer Emanuele Melisurgo of Bari, who obstinately sought to convince Ferdinando II to give his approval. But the king hesitated and once, in one of their discussions, almost as if he were defending himself from the seduction of Melisurgo's rhetoric, he dismissed him, saying, "Go, go away, otherwise like a woman I'll say yes to you." Finally, with the decree of April 16, 1855, the King granted Melisurgo the construction and operation of the train that would connect Naples with Brindisi. The engineer's project, however, was unsound: it planned to collect the necessary capital imagining that out of the three million inhabitants of the five provinces that the train would cross or skirt, they could find 55,000 people who would be able to underwrite four shares of 100 ducats a year, paid in very small installments over four years, yielding an interest rate of 12.25 percent as a maximum "hoped for," and guaranteeing a minimum of 5 percent. The reality of the matter was quite different: of the 55,000 shareholders foreseen, at the close of the public offering they hardly found 1,000. The failure of the enterprise was due to a number of factors: the real poverty of the provinces and greed; mistrust of entrepreneurial risk; the people of Foggia's envy of the engineer from Bari who had risen so high; the insufficient participation of the government in actively encouraging the project instead of guaranteeing its interest on the capital; and lastly, real technical deficiencies in the project as a whole. The construction site was inaugurated on March 11, 1856, on the Arenaccia road near the church of the Madonna delle Grazie, with the presence of Cardinal Carbonelli. Despite this, the works did not proceed, leaving only judicial after-effects that lasted some decades, with forensic battles that involved Melisurgio's son Giulio, who was also an engineer. The failure of this enterprise was attributed to the power of the very same Duke of Ventignano whom we have already encountered as a "national"—or even "international"—jettatore in Dumas' fictionalized biography.[6] Episodes and anecdotes of this sort punctuate every aspect of Neapolitan life in the dying Kingdom. It is no coincidence that the approach of the final catastrophe virtually

---

6.   See the anecdote in De Cesare (1908: 263ff., 341).

appears to have taken place under the omen of jettatura, with the last court ball canceled by the terrible Duke, and with the image of the King near his death, recalling the "faces" which he had encountered and the "eyes" that had "looked at him" during his last journey in the provinces of the Kingdom.

Epilogue

The analysis of the ethnographic documentation has demonstrated the survival of ancient bewitching binding in the rural areas of Southern Italy in connection with other similar magical elements, such as possession and exorcism, spells and counterspells. This analysis shows how binding, possession, exorcism, spells, and counterspells all have their origin in the precariousness of daily life, the enormous power of the negative, and the lack of prospects for a realistically-oriented action to deal with critical moments of existence. Above all, they arise from a psychological reflex of *being-acted-upon*, with the psychic risks associated with it. In these conditions, the magical moment takes on particular importance in that it satisfies the need for psychological reintegration through techniques that set the crisis within certain mythical-ritual horizons and hide the historicity of becoming and the awareness of individual responsibility, thereby creating a protected regime that enables one to face the power of the negative in history. From the ethnographic analysis we also see how the magical moment is not limited to low ceremonial magic, nor is it completely isolated with respect to the rest of cultural life, but is instead articulated in connections and intermediate formations that involve folk Catholicism and its particular Southern magical accents, even reaching the heart of the Catholic cult itself. Starting from the assumption that the persistence of the magical moment in a modern society stands as evidence of contradictions and arrests in development that should be sought in the hegemonic forms of cultural life themselves, the ethnographic analysis was followed by a more strictly historiographic analysis aimed at measuring the participation of Southern Italian high culture in the choice between magic and rationality from which modern civilization was born. The discussion dwelled on the fact that the Neapolitan Enlightenment scarcely participated in the explicit coming-to-awareness of this choice. On the contrary, among some Neapolitan Enlightenment thinkers in the late 1700s, the ideology of jettatura took shape as a singular, practical compromise between magic and rationality. Neapolitan jettatura was not a serious option, but rather a facetious ambiguity: nonetheless it was precisely this facetious ambiguity that became a characteristic custom, distinguishing jettatura from bewitching binding and natural magic. In comparison to the Anglo-French Enlightenment, the inner limit of the Neapolitan Enlightenment finds its justification in the history (or more precisely, the nonhistory) of the Kingdom of Naples. The Kingdom lingered on in the contradictions of a weak, semifeudal monarchy, while elsewhere city-state civilization flourished and the great national monarchies took shape. So when the Anglo-French Enlightenment was introduced in Naples, it did not find the social and political conditions of its countries of origin, and above all, it could not graft itself onto a rationalizing experience of a vigorous commercial and industrial middle class within the context of an expanding national monarchy. In Naples, Enlightened rationalism thus made its entrance in reaction to and in contradiction with a social structure and an existential regime that were dominated by irrationality, disorder, and chance. But they were also lacking adequate civil forces for propagating throughout society the antimagic polemic and the requirements of rationalizing life featured in the Enlightenment movement and consolidating them into custom. Moreover, especially in the countryside, the ancient binding of witchery and demonology persisted in connection with other magical themes of possession, spells, and exorcism. Through a series of intermediate nuances, it was equally connected to various pagan-Catholic syncretisms and the accentuated magical coloring of Southern Italian Catholicism. To the extent that it was preserved (and is still preserved today), this is a situation that constitutes an ideological and traditional reflection of a deficit of civil energy, in the modern sense of the word. The *being-acted-upon* that lies at the foundation of magic and the magical moment of religion in fact constitutes the individual and psychological offset of the limits of a civil and secular *agency* in a given society in a given period. Moreover, to the extent that such limits burden consciousness to the point of annihilating it as moral energy, it results in resorting to rather restricted mythic-ritual techniques that—in the final instance—harbor the magical moment's repairing and reintegrating function.

I cannot think of a better way to close this study than to recall a passage from *Storia come pensiero e come azione*, celebrating the ethos of human work at the center of civil life:

> If we wish to answer the question what is the end of moral activity, and if in doing so we put aside the theological doctrine of obedience to commandments imposed by a personal god, and if we convert into its opposite the doctrine of the pessimists who, denying life, seek the end in mortification of the will to life until they annihilate it in asceticism or universal suicide, then the answer is that the object of morals is to promote life. "Long live the creator of life!" as Goethe sang.
>
> Life is promoted by all forms of spiritual activity with their works of truth, beauty, and practical utility. By means of them reality is contemplated and understood, the earth is covered with the cultivated fields and industries, families arise, states are founded, battles fought, blood spilt, there is victory and there is progress. . . . Good and evil, with their contrasts, the triumph of good and the renewal of undermining threats and danger, are not the efforts of intervention by a power extraneous to life, even though they appear as such in mythological representations of a tempting seductive devil; they are to be found in life itself—in fact, they are life itself. . . . The kind of action which sets the boundaries of each separate activity, which makes them specifically fulfill their own proper office, which thus prevents the disintegration of spiritual unity and guarantees liberty, the kind which faces and combats evil in all its forms and gradations; it is called moral activity. (Croce 1941: 42ff)[1]

This magnanimous exhortation to life and liberty should be placed alongside the sublime Homeric episode in which Thetis and Achilles, embracing Patroclus' corpse, carry the shining shield on which the hero contemplates a series of scenes depicting natural and civil order,

---

1.   English edition translated by Sylvia Sprigge (1949: 55–57). —Trans.

circumscribed by the Ocean's currents. Upon seeing these images governed by the degree of human work, the hero opens himself up to his heroic destiny and rises up trembling: "Now I shall arm myself for war!" For the Southern Italians, too, it is necessary to abandon the sterile embrace of the corpses of their history and open themselves to a heroic destiny that is higher and more modern than what they had in the past. This is a destiny that is not a fantastic city of the sun to be found in the Calabrian mountains,[2] but a civil, earthly city solely entrusted to the ethos of human work, and conspiring with other earthly cities scattered throughout this old Europe and the wider world of which Europe is a child. To the extent that this will take place, the kingdom of obscurity and shadows will be chased back within its boundaries—the Ocean's currents of the Homeric episode—and it will cause the specious light of magic to fade, a light that uncertain men in an insecure society, for practical motives of existence, substituted for the authentic light of reason.

---

2.   A reference to Tommaso Campanella's *The city of the sun* ([1602] 1981).—Trans.

Appendix: On Apulian tarantism

Every year, from June 29th to 30th, the *tarantolati*[1] of the region meet in the Chapel of St. Paul in Galatina, giving rise to the episodes that our friend André Martin has captured in some very interesting photographs. The Christianized form of Galatina's *tarantolismo* recalls the pagan version that formed part of the magical therapies of possession at one time quite common in Apulia. Around the end of the seventeenth century, Reverend Domenico Sangenito wrote about the pagan form in a letter to Antonio Bulifon, a French bookseller in Naples whose name occupies a relatively significant place in the development of the new Neapolitan culture (on Bulifon, see Nicolini 1932: 16ff.). Sangenito, whose letter to Bulifon is contained in *Lettere memorabilia istoriche politiche ed erudite* (1693), was an attentive eyewitness to what he refers, and this gives his report particular worth. The following is an essential excerpt:

---

1. The notes in this appendix are a prelude to de Martino's magisterial ethnography, *La terra del rimorso* (1961, English ed. 2005, *The land of remorse*). In the preliminary phase of this research project as we see it here, de Martino uses the terms *tarantolismo* and *tarantolati* to indicate the condition and its sufferers, but he later adopted the alternative denominations of *tarantism* and *tarantati*, which are now considered to be the standard forms. In the excerpt from Sangenito below, another archaic term for the afflicted is *attarantato*. —Trans.

Those who suffer the bite of the tarantula, after a few hours complain in an inarticulate voice, and if the people around them ask what is afflicting them, they do not offer very much in the way of a reply but simply look back at them with a sinister eye; others gesture by placing a hand on their hearts. In this way, as the inhabitants of those towns are experienced persons, they immediately recognize the illness tormenting them, so without delay they call for musicians of various instruments, because some dance to the sound of the guitar, others to the zither, and still others to the sound of a violin. As the musicians strike up the music, little by little they begin to dance; they ask for swords, and though they are not swordsmen, they handle them like masters. They also ask for mirrors, and while they gaze at themselves in them, they let out innumerable high-pitched sighs. They want ribbons, chains, fancy clothing, and when these have been brought, they accept them with inexplicable happiness, and with great reverence they thank those who have brought them. They lay out all of these aforementioned things in order around the stockade, where they dance from time to time engaging one another, according to the stimulus that the illness gives them. They begin the dance an hour after sunrise and finish an hour before noon, without ever resting, except when an instrument gets out of tune. At that point, they breathe impatiently until the instrument is placed back in tune, noting with wonder how such rough and uncouth people as are those who cultivate the land, shepherds and similar country-folk, have such a fine knowledge of the consonance and dissonance of musical instruments; they are as much distressed by them as they are satisfied by them. An hour later they begin the dance anew, continuing until sundown in the same fashion without tiring. Among the many that I saw, they never had more than three days of suffering if their illness was given a remedy with sound. Others have needed to follow the dance for eight, even ten days. While they are dancing they are out of their senses, and they do not distinguish relative or friend, but all are the same to them. It is quite true that at times they invite some elegant and graceful youth to dance. The furnishings that they use are usually of an indefinite color like flesh—pink, red, cerulean blue and the like; when they see black, they become so angry that they charge at someone wearing it, chasing him away. To my knowledge, there was only one among the many who did not dislike black cloth: this one jumped with as much vigor as the others, but in a more agitated manner.

Sangenito then passes to relating two particular cases he witnessed:

> Giovan Giacomo Teforo (whom I saw dance more than six times) one day was in a forest for his business, and I believe he realized that the time had come to pay tribute to his mortifying tarantula. He headed toward the village but was found on the road, lying on the ground naked. When this was known in the hometown we shared, many ran to his aid. We found the miserable peasant oppressed with difficult breathing, and we observed moreover that his face and hands had begun to turn black. Since his illness was known to all, a guitar was brought whose harmony was immediately accepted by him. He began first to move his feet, then shortly thereafter his legs; he supported himself on his knees, and shortly after he rose to a walk. Finally in the space of a quarter of an hour, he was dancing in such a way that he rose three palms off the ground. He sighed, but with such fury that he terrified those present, and within an hour the black from his hands and face went away, and he regained his original color. In the castle of Motta di Montecorvino, I had the occasion to see five *attarantati* dance at the same time and inside of the same stockade: they were four plough-men and a beautiful country lass. I observed new things in this union, as each had taken an alias from among the names of ancient kings, no less. Some were related to each other by kinship, and they treated one another in such a way that reciprocal affection was observed, and compliments were reiterated to the great admiration of the spectators. They happily per-formed the usual course of dance over three days; the last evening, before taking leave, they politely asked for a squadron of men at arms. They were given ten harquebusiers, who were divided into two rings, ready to fire a salvo. They then asked for a glass of water and a little powdered salt, both of which were brought. The chief, or as we might call him, the ideal King of the Kings (his name was Pietro Boccamazza) drew a sign in the water in the form of a Cross, they each took some of this water, signaled to the squadron to leave, and with a deep bow they said, "We will see each other next year." After so much fatigue those wretches did not remember a single thing, but in the midst of the multitude of people they saw surrounding them, they only begged to be taken home.

From this report one can surmise the features of Apulian tar-antism in the second half of the seventeenth century with sufficient approximation. The crisis appears to be characterized by a condition of deep melancholic depression, of dullness, or—to judge from the case of Teforo—a fall to the ground related to hysteria or epilepsy; the "cure" consisted above all in the use of certain musical rhythms that had the function of releasing the psychic block, stimulating a hint of mania-cal agitation, and leading this agitation back into the institutional path of a jumping dance, repeated for three days from dawn to dusk, with an interruption of an hour in the middle of the day. As the episode of tarantism at Castle of Motta di Montecorvino demonstrates, this dance could have a figured movement, representing a sort of mimicked dream followed by complete oblivion upon reawakening. The event took place in a stockade to which the tarantati were led and where their pantomime was supported and directed by the sound of guitars, zith-ers, or violins. Sangenito's report receives the belief that the crisis—for which tarantism represents an institutionalized and socialized system of treatment—is caused by the bite of the tarantula: but this insect has nothing to do whatsoever with this situation, if only in mythic fantasy, inasmuch as being bitten by the tarantula is only an imagination or even a hallucinatory experience that gives a horizon and figure to a crisis of a clearly psychic nature. Apulian tarantism—which survives in Chris-tianized forms in the feast-day of Saint Paul in Galatina—has numer-ous historical-religious parallels, especially in shamanistic magic. In his monograph *Le traitement de la manie dans les mystères de Dionysos et des Corybantes* (1949: 64ff.), H. Jeanmaire highlights a group of practices of this type throughout a vast area that embraces the Islamic countries of Mediterranean Africa and even extends into the Arabian peninsula, Sudan, and Abyssinia:

> They are practices of a popular sort, performed by elements belonging to the lowest strata of the population without being limited to them, especially in regard to the female population. We are in the presence of disciples who service a particular cult not to a principal divinity, but to a host of hierarchically ordered spirits. These spirits manifest them-selves through the state of possession during séances given by the con-gregations. This state is accompanied by consecutive trances into which the disciple falls, and it is translated into frenetic dances to which the possessed person abandons himself. Moreover, this is a state whose

appearance and disappearance are prepared and provoked, to a certain extent on command, by appropriate gymnastics (in general with oscillations and spins of the torso and head) and also by the suggestion of certain rhythms. [...] In exorcism proper, which is practiced in an environment in which possession is understood as the effect of the intrusion of a naturally maleficent spirit, the exorcism tends to expel the evil entity. In the (supposed or suggested) states of possession considered here, however, we may correctly characterize the process by observing that the method of treatment used aims not so much to suppress the affective and delirious states but rather to transform such states through the elimination of their depressive factor and utilize them in view of creating a new equilibrium of the personality. This equilibrium is achieved by virtue of a form of symbiosis with the possessing spirit, who is transformed into a protecting spirit, and by virtue of a normalization of the crisis state in the form of the trance provoked.

The relationship with tarantism is clear: the state of crisis, the trance induced and commanded by "performance directors," the ordering function of the musical rhythm, the dance, the need to periodically repeat the practice, and especially the "cure" as ritual control of a crisis. Without the ritual's control, the crisis would oscillate between poles of melancholic depression and maniacal excitation, which form the characteristic features of tarantism just as it appears in Sangenito's description. As for the possessing spirits, Sangenito certainly makes no mention of them. One should note, however, that the imaginary or hallucinatory tarantula takes the place of a spirit of this sort, and the pantomime of the Castle of Motta di Montecorvino must have had a socially recognized and accepted meaning, as would appear from the agreement and coordination among the four tarantati during the recitation, which moreover seems supported by the audience as if it were a well-known event. From Sangenito's report the meaning of the "acted" myth is undoubtedly impossible to reconstruct, but the obscurity is likely attributable to the nature of the document, which limits itself to sketching some of most outward and spectacular features of the mimicry.

With regard to the function of techniques of this sort, we should note that at least an intuition of the correct solution is to be found as early as Plato's *Laws*, where in discussing the regulation of exercises that should develop the souls of youths, he makes reference to the cures of Corybantes:

> Both these conditions [in Corybantic possession and in children] are a species of fear, and fear is the result of some inadequacy in the personality. When one treats such condition by vigorous movement, this external motion, by canceling out the internal agitation that gives rise to the fear [*phobos*] and frenzy [*mania*], induces, after all the painful thumping of the heart experienced by each patient, a feeling of calm and peace in his soul. The result is very gratifying. Whereas the wakeful children are sent to sleep, the revelers (far from asleep!) by being set to dance to the music of the pipes, are restored to mental health after their derangement, with the assistance of the gods to whom they sacrifice so propitiously.[2]

Elsewhere (*Phaedrus*, 244–245 a) Plato distinguishes between madness and ορϑη μανια, that is, between a "right madness" that takes place in initiation rites that are carried out correctly and that is "right" in that—as Jeanmaire notes, *Dionysos* 1951, p. 138—it refers to practices that basically consist of "regulating the onset of madness by giving it a telestic orientation" (cf. Linforth 1946b: 163–72). On the basis of these considerations, Apulian tarantism merits a careful historical-religious analysis, both in the pagan-type forms depicted in Sangenito's report, as well as in the process of its Christian reabsorption, of which a trace is still alive in the events taking place during the feast of Saint Paul in Galatina.

---

2.   From the translation by Trevor J. Saunders (1997: 1461), in *Plato: Complete works*. —Trans.

References

Alexander of Aphrodisias. 1990. *Ethical problems*. London: Duckworth.

Amabile, Luigi. 1882. "Consultazione o arbitrii sopra l'aumento delle entrate del Regno di Napoli." In *Fra Tommaso Campanella ne' Castelli di Napoli*, vol. II, Documento 199. Naples.

Andrews, I. G. 1897. "Neapolitan witchcraft," *Folklore* 8: 1–9.

Angelini, Pietro. 2008. *Ernesto de Martino*. Rome: Carocci.

Barb, A. 1926. *Akademie der Wissenschaften: Der Römische Limes in Österreich*. Issue 16. Vienna: Leipzig, Hölder-Pichler-Tempsky AG.

Bartmann, Bernhard. (1932) 1956. *Teologia dogmatica*. Italian translation of *Lehrbuch der Dogmatik*. Alba: Ed. Paoline.

Bonomo, Giuseppe. 1953. *Scongiuri del popolo siciliano*. Palermo: Palumbo.

Brouette, Emile. 1948. *La civilization chrétienne du XVI siècle devant le problem satanique*. Paris: Les Etudes Carmelitaines.

Bruno, Giordano. (1590) 1998. *De Magia*. Translated as "On Magic" in *Cause, principle, and unity*. Edited by Robert de Lucca, Richard J. Blackwell, and Alfonso Ingegno. Cambridge: Cambridge University Press.

Campanella, Tomasso. (1602) 1981. *The city of the sun: A poetical dialogue*. Translated by Daniel J. Donno. Berkeley: University of California Press.

———. 1620. *Del senso delle cose e della magia*, Book IV. Frankfurt.

Cione, Edmundo. 1942. *Napoli romantica*. Milan: Morano Editore.

Croce, Benedetto. (1941) 1949. *History as the story of liberty*. Translated by Sylvia Sprigge. London: George Allen and Unwin Limited.

———. 1945. "La cicalata di Nicola Valletta." *Quaderni di Critica* no. 3.

———. (1925). 1970. *History of the kingdom of Naples.* Translated by Frances Frenaye. Chicago: University of Chicago Press.

De Cesare, Raffaele. 1908. *La fine di un Regno,* I. Città di Castello: S. Lapi.

de Félice, Philippe. 1947. *Foules en délire, extases collectives.* Paris: Albin Michel.

De Jorio. 1832. *Mimica degli antichi investigate nel gestire napoletano.* Naples: Fibreno.

de Martino, Ernesto. 1958. *Morte e pianto rituale nel mondo antico: Dal lamento funebre antico al pianto di Maria.*Turin: Bollati Boringhieri.

———. (1959) 2005. *The land of remorse: A study of Southern Italian tarantism.* Translated and annotated by Dorothy Louise Zinn. London: Free Association Books.

———. 1977. *La fine del mondo: Contributo all'analisi delle apocalissi culturali.* Edited by Clara Gallini. Turin: Einaudi.

———. 1995a. *Note di campo: Spedizione in Lucania 30 Sett–31 Ott. 1952.* Edited by Clara Gallini. Lecce: Argo.

———. 1995b. *Storia e metastoria. I fondamenti di una teoria del sacro.* Edited by Marcello Massenzio with an introduction by Marcello Massenzio. Lecce: Argo.

———. 1996. *L'Opera a cui lavoro: Apparato critico e documentario alla "Spedizione etnologica" in Lucania.* Edited by Clara Gallini. Lecce: Argo.

———. (1956) 2012. "Crisis of presence and religious reintegration." Translated by Tobia Farnetti and Charles Stewart. *HAU Journal of Ethnographic Theory* 2 (2): 434–50.

de Tonquedec, Joseph. 1938. *Les maladies nerveuses et mentales et les manifestations diaboliques.* Paris: Beauchesne.

Dumas, Alexandre. (1889) 1950. *Corricolo.* Paris: Calman Lévy. Italian translation by Gino Doria. Naples: Ricciardi.

Dumas, Georges. 1947. *Le surnaturel et les dieux après les maladies mentales.* Paris: Presses Universitaires de France.

Eliade, Mircea. 1949. *Le mythe de l'éternel retour.* Paris: Gallimard.

———. 1951. *Le chamanisme.* France: Payot.

Elsworthy, F. T. 1895. *The evil eye.* London: Murray.

Ferrari, Fabrizio M. 2012. *Ernesto de Martino on religion: The crisis and the presence*. Sheffield: Equinox.

Finichel, Otto. 1951. *Trattato di psicanalisi*. Editions Astrolabe Ubaldinis.

Gallini, Clara, and Francesco Faeta, eds. 1999. *I viaggi nel sud di Ernesto de Martino*. Turin: Bollati Boringhieri.

Garin, Eugenio. 1954. *Medioevo e Rinascimento*. Bari: Laterza and Figli.

Giannone, Pietro. 1844. *Storia civile del regno di Napoli*. Milan: Borroni e Scotti.

Gifford, Edward S. 1958. *The evil eye*. New York: The Macmillan Company.

Heliodorus. 1967. *An Aethiopian history written in Greek by Heliodorus*. Translated by Thomas Underdown. New York: AMS Press.

Janet, Pierre. 1926–28. *De l'angoisse à l'extase*. 2 vols. Paris: Librairie Félix Alcan.

Jeanmaire, H. 1949. "Le traitement de la manie dans les mystères de Dionysos et des Corybantes." *Journal de Psycologie* 42: 64–82.

———. 1951. *Dionysos*. Paris: Payot.

Krause, Johann. 1951. *Hexen unter uns*. Hamburg: Verl. Hamburgische Bücherei.

La Sorsa, Saverio. 1915. "Superstizioni, pregiudizi e credenze popolari pugliesi." *Estratto da Lares, Bullettino della Società di Etnografia Italiana* 4 (1): 49–67.

Lhermitte, Jean. (1956) 1957. *Vrais et faux possédés*. Italian translation. Paris: A. Fayard.

Linforth, Ivan M. 1946a. *The corybantic rites in Plato. University of California Publications in Classical Philology* 13 (5): 121–62.

———. 1946b. *Telestic madness in Plato, Phaedrus 244 d-e. University of California Publications in Classical Philology* 13 (6): 163–72.

Magliocco, Sabina. 2009. "Italian cunning craft: Some preliminary observations." *Journal for the Academic Study of Magic* 5: 103–33.

Mancini, E. 1887. "Jettatura e scongiuro." *Nuova Antologia* 12 (3): 607–72.

Manzoni, Alessandro. (1827) 1972. *The betrothed*. Translated by Bruce Penman. London: Penguin.

Marugi, Gian Leonardo. 1788. *Pastore arcade di Numero, Capricci sul fascino*. Naples.

Massenzio, Marcello. 1997. "La Ripetizione della ripetizione." In *Ernesto de Martino nella cultura europea*, edited by Clara Gallini and Marcello Massenzio, 237–46. Naples: Liguori.

Maussbach, Joseph. (1954) 1957. *Teologia morale*. Italian translation of *Katholische Moraltheologie*. Münster: Aschendorff.

Mayer, Karl August. 1840. *Neapel und die Neapolitaner oder Briefe aus Neapel in die Heimat*. Oldenburg: Schulze.

Niccolini, Fausto. 1932. *La giovinezza di Giambiattista Vico*. Bari.

———. 1937. *Peste e Untori nei Promessi Sposi e nella realtà storica*. Bari: Laterza and Figli.

Oesterreich, Traugott Konstantin. 1922. *Die Besessenheit*. Halle: Langensalza, Wendt, and Klauwell.

Palumbo, Cosimo. 1935. *Scrittori della jettatura*. Rome: Casa.

Pàstina, Roberto. 2005. "Il concetto di presenza nel primo de Martino." In *Ernesto de Martino e la formazione del suo pensiero*, edited by Clara Gallini, 115–29. Naples: Liguori.

Paulain, Augustin. 1906. *Des graces d'oraison: Traité de théologie mystique*. 5th edition. Paris: G. Beauchesne.

Pauly, August Friedrich von, Georg Wissowa, Wilhelm Kroll, and Konrat Ziegler. 1894. *Paulys Real-Encyclopädie der classischen Altertumswissenschaft*. Stuttgart: J. B. Metzler.

Peterson, Erik. 1926. ΕΙΣΘΕΟΣ, *Epigraphische, formgeschichtliche und religionsgeschichtliche Untersuchungen*. Göttingen.

Pitzurra, Mario. 1957. "Considerazioni tratte da un viaggio di studio su un piccolo paese della Lucania." In *Bollettino FIMI* no. 6.

Plutarch. 1909. "Symposiacs." In *The complete works of Plutarch: Essays and miscellanies*. Vol. 3. New York: Crowell.

Pradel, Fritz. 1907. *Griechische und süditalienische Gebete, Beschwörungen und Rezepte des Mittelalters*. Religionsgeschichtliche Versuche und Vorarbeiten. Giessen: Töpelmann.

Praz, Mario. 1942. *La carne la morte e il diavolo nella letteratura romantica*, Turin: Sansoni.

Rehfues, P. J. 1808. *Gemälde von Neapel und seine Umgebung*. Zürich.

Reitzenstein, Richard. 1926. "Ein christliches Zauberbuch und seine Vorlage." *Archive für Religionswissenschaft* 24: 176–78.

Riviera, Cesare Della. 1986. *Mondo magico*. Edizioni Mediterranee.

Roland, A. 1845. *Sketches of Naples*. Philadelphia: E. Ferrett and Company.

Rolfe, Eustace Neville, and Holcombe Ingleby. 1888. *Neapel in 1888.* London.

Rossi, Paolo.1957 (1968). *Francis Bacon: From magic to science.* Translated by Sacha Rabinovitch. Chicago: University of Chicago Press.

Sangenito, Domenico. 1693. *Lettere memorabilia istoriche politiche ed erudite.* Naples.

Saunders, Trevor J. 1997. *Plato: Complete works.* Edited by John M. Cooper. Indianapolis: Hackett.

Schäfer, Herbert, and H. Wendte. 1955. *Hexenmacht und Hexenjagd.* Hamburg: Verlag für kriminalistische Fachliteratur.

Schioppa, A. 1832. *Antidoto al fascino detto volgarmente jettatura.* Naples: Fibreno.

Schmidt, Phillip. 1956. *Dunkle Mächte: Ein Buch von Aberglauben einst und Heute.* Frankfurt: Knecht.

Seligmann, Siegfried. 1910. *Der böse Blick und Verwandtes: Ein Beitrag zur Geschichte des Aberglaubens aller Zeiten und Völker.* Berlin: Bersdorf.

Soldan, Wilhelm Gottlieb and Heinrich Heppe. 1911. *Geschichte der Hexenprozesse.* Stuttgart: J. G. Cotta.

Spencer, Walter Baldwin, and Frances James Gillen. 1927. *The Aranda.* New York: Macmillan.

Strehlow, Carl. 1907–20. *Die Aranda und Loritia-Stämmen in Zentral-Australien.* Veröff. Aus dem städt. Völker-Museum. Frankfurt am Main: Joseph Baer and Co.

Talamonti, Adelina. 2005. "La labilità della persona magica." In *Ernesto de Martino e la formazione del suo pensiero*, edited by Clara Gallini, 79–114. Naples: Liguori.

Tambornino, Julius. 1909. "De antiquorum daemonismo." In *Religiongeschichtliche Versuche und Vorarbeiten* 3, booklet 3. Giessen.

Tanquerey, Adolphe. 1928. *Compendio di teologia ascetica e mistica.* Paris: Desclée and Co.

———. 1957. *Enciclopedia liturgica.* Alba: Ed. Paoline.

Thorndike, Lynn.1929–1941. *A history of magic and experimental science.* 6 volumes. New York: Columbia University Press.

Trede, Theodor. 1889–1891. *Das Heidentum in der römischen Kirche: Bilder aus dem religiösen und sittlichen Leben Süditaliens.* 4 volumes. Gothe: F.A. Perthes.

Tuchmann, Jules. 1884–85. "La fascination." In *La fascination: Extraits de Mélusine.* Paris: H. Gaidoz & E. Rolland.

Vagheggini, Cipriano. 1957. *Il senso teologico della liturgia.* Rome: Ed. Paoline.

Valletta, Nicola. 1787. *Cicalata sul fascino, volgarmente detto jettatura.* Naples: Michele Morelli.

van der Leeuw, Gerardus. 1933. "Die sogenannte epische Einleitung der Zauberformeln." *Zeitschrift für Religionspsychologie* 6 (4): 161–80.

———. 1956. *Phänomenologie der Religion*, Tübingen: Verlag von J. C. B. Mohr.

Wagner, Max Leopold. 1913. "Il malocchio e credenze affini in Sardegna." *Estratto da Lares, Bullettino della Società di Etnografia Italiana* 2 (2–3): 129–50.

Webster, Hutton. 1948. *Magic: A sociological study.* Redwood City, CA: Stanford University Press.

Wilby, Emma. 2009. *Cunning folk and familiar spirits: Shamanistic visionary traditions in early modern British witchcraft and magic.* Brighton: Sussex Academic Press.

Zezza, Baron Michele. 1835. *La Jettatura poemma cuommeco de lo Barone Michele Zezza* Naples: Società Filomatica.

Index

Hau Books is committed to publishing the most distinguished texts in classic and advanced anthropological theory. The titles aim to situate ethnography as the prime heuristic of anthropology, and return it to the forefront of conceptual developments in the discipline. *Hau* Books is sponsored by some of the world's most distinguished anthropology departments and research institutions, and releases its titles in both print editions and open-access formats.

www.haubooks.com

Supported by

HAU-N. E. T.
Network of Ethnographic Theory

University of Aarhus – EPICENTER (DK)
University of Amsterdam (NL)
University of Bergen (NO)
Brown University (US)
California Institute of Integral Studies (US)
University of Canterbury (NZ)
University of Chicago (US)
University of Colorado Boulder Libraries (US)
CNRS – Centre d'Études Himalayennes (FR)
Cornell University (US)
University of Edinburgh (UK)
The Graduate Institute, Geneva Library (CH)
University of Helsinki (FL)
Johns Hopkins University (US)
University of Kent (UK)
Lafayette College Library (US)
Institute of Social Sciences of the University of Lisbon (PL)
University of Manchester (UK)
The University of Manchester Library (UK)
Museu Nacional – UFRJ (BR)
Norwegian Museum of Cultural History (NO)
University of Oslo (NO)
University of Oslo Library (NO)
Pontificia Universidad Católica de Chile (CL)
Princeton University (US)
University of Queensland (AU)
University of Rochester (US)
Universidad Autónoma de San Luis Potosi (MX)
University of Sydney (AU)

www.haujournal.org/haunet

www.ingramcontent.com/pod-product-compliance
Ingram Content Group UK Ltd.
Pitfield, Milton Keynes, MK11 3LW, UK
UKHW051633280525
459017UK00013B/517